The Origi

Ask A Player
Volume 1

Ask a Player

"White Folks comes out blazing razor sharp wit from both barrels riding a horse called The Butt Naked Truth."

Cover designed by: Mr. Sharpgame Chief consultant for G.a.m.e. to the Game Films.

We now proudly offer: Graphic Design, Photography, Video Editing, Commercials and Full Music Video Production to the public.

Contact us at: 909.562.8174 or 1.866.376.9941
www.mr.sharpgame@yahoo.com

All Photos by: Martypix.com
Capture The Moments Photography
Las Vegas' premier photographer
[702] 205.0874

The Original White Folks

Ask a Player

Preserving the Game one book and one answer at a time

Compiled and Edited by Essila Ringer

The Original White Folks

Folks' Disclaimer: If I offend anyone in the course of giving real talk, player's answers to the following questions, I would like to sincerely say…
You can Kiss My ASS!

COMING SOON!
One of the most powerful series ever written on Game law, conduct and etiquette.

A collaboration by:

The Original White Folks, Rosebudd Bitterdose and Mr. Sharpgame.

Over 100 years of hard fought knowledge and experience from three generations.

Ignorance of the law is no excuse!

Ask a Player

Copyright © January 2008 by:
Darryel A.Woodson   a/k/a
The Original White Folks

Available on: www.Amazon.com
www.Barnes&Noble.com

ISBN: 978-0-9837476-0-4

1st Printing: November, 2011

Published By:

Players Publishing
P.O. Box 162610
Atlanta, Georgia 30321
askaplayer@gmail.com

www.facebook.com/originalwhitefolks
www.youtube.com/originalwhitefolks
www.myspace.com/originalwhitefolks

The Original White Folks

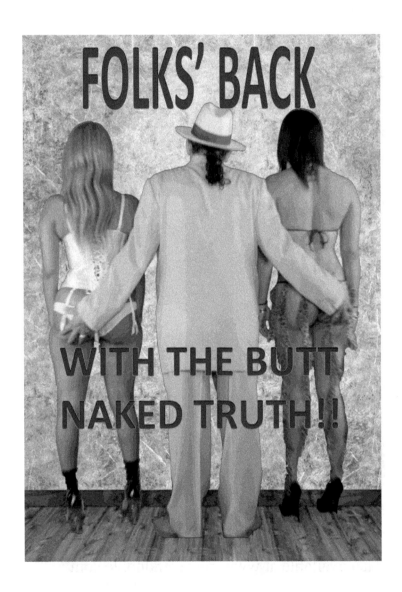

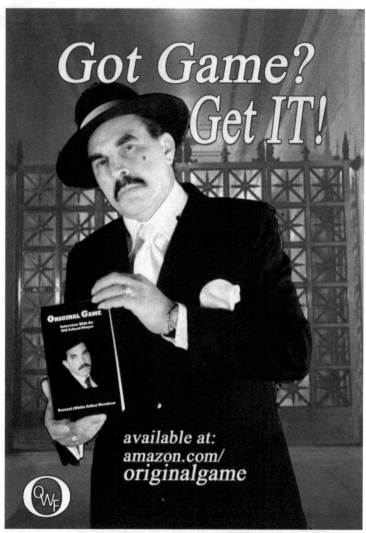

The Original White Folks

DEDICATIONS

This book is dedicated to following persons:

My mother Marie (Droopy) Woodson. Marie was a player. I got a head start in the game because I was born in... not sworn in.

My uncle, Charles (Rocky) Reed. Rocky gave me time honored, real game in my teen-aged years and still provides an occasional profound gem of wisdom.

My grandfather, George (Sweet Papa) Barnes. Sweet Papa raised me from childhood. Sweet Papa taught me life skills and provided the wisdom and knowledge necessary to make the transition from boyhood to manhood.

My grandmother, Cora Barnes, was a stabilizing force in my life. Cora loved, nurtured, encouraged and guided me through an extremely difficult childhood. My grandmother's uncanny wit helped spawn my sharp tongue and affinity for realism. Cora always knew the right thing to say and exactly when to say it.

My daughter, Jakneka Miller. Jakneka has more access to me than most, yet she does not ask for THE BUTT NAKED TRUTH. I wish she would.

My friend, partner, co-defendant & mentor since the 1960s. Ronald T. Jenkins, better known by his friends as "JINX" Jinx died in a Georgia prison serving a life sentence for a murder he didn't commit… He refused to testify on the guilty one. Rest in peace my friend.

My friend and Player to the end Danny Boy. RIP

In loving memory of Celeste (Cee Cee) Thompson.

The Original White Folks

ACKNOWLEDGEMENTS

I wish to thank and acknowledge the following persons, without their friendship, faith and assistance this book would not have been possible:

Anthony Sanders, Editor-in-Chief of *The St. Louis Metro Evening Whirl*. Anthony had the courage and vision to be the first to carry my **Ask a Player** column in his newspaper.

Marcus Williams, owner of Nubian Bookstore at Southlake Mall in Morrow, Georgia. After reading several **Ask a Player** columns and sharing them with some of his customers, Marcus encouraged me to compile my columns into book form. Marcus' encouragement and assistance with my books has been invaluable.

Amber Chase. Amber is a screenplay writer that compiled, edited and typed the original **Ask a**

Player newspaper column. Without Amber's assistance in the beginning there may not have been a column. We were up many long nights meeting my deadline. Amber had faith in me.

Essila Ringer, whose dedication, expert editing and formatting skills transformed **Ask a Player,** the newspaper column, into **Ask a Player,** the book. This woman is awesome!

My friend, **Dr. Mark Williams**, formally known in the streets as **"Big Silk"**, of Right Path Youth Foundation and Right Path Entertainment, Record and Film Corp. Minister Williams made a special effort to effect the introduction of Anthony Sanders and myself. Therefore, in all honesty, if it were not for Dr. Williams' efforts, I would have been at a loss for a vehicle to carry my **Ask a Player** column forward.

Last, but by no means least, **my friend**, partner and CEO of Atlanta based Godfather Enterprises, (GFE Digital Media) and Godfather Studios (Audio/Video). This brother has helped in more ways than I can count... **Bishop**

Special Acknowledgements:

Erikka Tiffani, brand marketer, who tirelessly worked on the marketing, advertising and production of this book, the **Ask a Player** column as well as directing and editing my initial **Ask a Player** Youtube episodes. Erikka is a technical and entertainment powerhouse, she possesses a wealth of information, ability and skills.

Angel Hull, marketing executive, realtor, model/actress who has worked in multiple capacities on all of my projects. I do not have enough time/space to say all that needs to be said about Angel…

Carlton Cadillac Brandon, my friend, has played an integral part in all of my projects. This man's time and dedication is immeasurable. An excellent actor, speaker, writer & he is a Chef!

My Pimp friend **Tony Mac** for the realness of it.

IF KNOWLEDGE IS POWER
GAME IS A NUCLEAR BOMB!

NOTE TO READERS

This publication is a compilation of questions and answers taken from my newspaper/magazine columns entitled **Ask A Player.** The columns appeared in both the St. Louis Metro Evening Whirl and Atlanta Metro Weekly Whirl newspapers as well as **Street Elements** magazine. The questions and answers are real. The names have been changed to protect the "innocent." Any similarity to real persons, other than myself, either living or dead is purely coincidental. This book is for entertainment only.

Angel Hull   Carlton Cadillac Brandon

INTRODUCTION

Ask a Player provides totally realistic, profoundly accurate answers and solutions to what has become an ever-increasing misinformed, misguided and undecided society. Problems and issues of concern for the everyday person have become increasingly more difficult to address or understand. Real life and fantasy have become entwined with one another. The average citizen is losing the ability to navigate through the literal maze of bullshit that faces them daily.

American people, especially those of us in "the hood", have been hoodwinked, bamboozled and led astray by advances in technology, fantasies and falsehoods perpetrated by motion pictures and the music industry; Hollywood-styled, commercial religion, drugs, homosexuality, HIV/AIDS, HPV, murder, an un-winnable war, poverty, government and church scandals. The list goes on. Meanwhile, Corporate America is turning a profit from it all. Our people have become caught-up in confusion and misdirection, while trying to live the so-called "American Dream." We as a people have lost sight of what's **really** going on.

For decades, written media, television, Hollywood and, more recently, the music industry have characterized, portrayed and misrepresented pimps and players as inarticulate, overdressed clowns, suckers, buffoons and snitches. In part, my motivation to write the **Ask a Player** newspaper/magazine columns and resulting book is to help dispel the age-old falsehoods, myths and mysteries surrounding the nature of pimps and players; I provide real answers, workable solutions and guidance to real life situations, questions and concerns. **Ask a Player** also offers a public look into the otherwise private rules, regulations and thoughts of an educated, well-traveled polished player.

As a lifetime player, in the face of pimp and player reputations at stake, I feel a duty to provide well thought out, common sense answers. These answers are rooted in the original rules of the game; Time-honored original game that has been passed down from one generation of players to the next.

Understand that players operate on absolute stark reality. (The Butt Naked Truth) Players are not handcuffed by the limitations imposed on the rest of society by laws, morality, religion and the desire for social acceptability. We think and live outside of the box. Therefore, answers to the questions in my columns/books will afford the average person an opportunity to obtain the prospective of someone who has lived life in the raw, undiluted **real** world without limitations or pretences.

Readers are provided an opportunity to make realistic decisions and distinguish real life from fantasy, based upon forty + years of wisdom, knowledge and experience from a real player. Ask A Player provides real advice, from a real player who has seen and done it all. It's all just super-sized, plain ole common sense…which by the way, is not common at all.

Dear Player,

Why does a hoe need a pimp? She already has all the tools necessary to do her job. It's not like rocket science or anything.

-Sharonda 23, St. Louis, MO

Dear Have All Your Tools,

The answer to this question will most likely take up all of my allotted space because it is much too profound, involved and technical to attempt a short answer. Since this question is asked of me more than any other, I will give it my best shot, while trying to be brief. Keep in mind that this is a newspaper column and I have limited space in which to write. Thus, I can only scratch the surface here. A detailed answer to this and other frequently asked questions will be found in my up-coming DVDs.

First off, let me make an analogy to properly answer this question. Let's take something that most people can grasp or identify with, Income tax. Why does the average taxpayer need H&R Block? They have their W-2 form, 1040 tax return form, a calculator, pen and paper, all the tools necessary to do the job. I'll tell you why, the people at H&R Block are experts, with many years of training, knowledge and experience. They know moves of which the average person would never think. H&R Block knows how to get a taxpayer maximum money without breaking the rules and risking prosecution. If a taxpayer does their own tax return, they are most likely to miss some steps, short themselves out of money that's due them, and may end up in jail. There are intricate complicated steps to be taken to get top dollar. If you don't know these moves exist, you can't use them to get paid. That's why the guidance, direction and instruction of a professional in the field, are necessary to achieve maximum return for the work you put in. Like H&R Block, pimps have offices in all 50 states, one near year you.

Pimps wear many hats. (No pun intended). Pimps provide unseen and rarely thought of services to hos. A pimp necessarily has to be a lawyer, psychologist, psychiatrist, medical doctor, hair and make-up consultant, wardrobe coordinator, consumer guide, etiquette and social graces instructor. Pimps are business and financial managers as well. Pimps invest money, flip cars, houses, etc. Thus, any money a real pimp has is invested and grows. Other duties include, but are not limited to, transportation, event planning, travel arrangements, computer training and web page design. Negotiating employment with Nevada brothels, Bunny Ranch, etc, escort services, design and placement of ads in adult magazines are also necessary.

Of course, having a web site includes marketing and advertising, business cards, flyers, etc. These and a host of other skills are standard operating procedure for pimps. Professional prostitutes cannot do without these services. Keep in mind that we are discussing *professional pimps*, not suckers and lames who label themselves pimps because they have a girl friend that sells pussy, owns a pimp cup and a shinny suit or two. *Actually, they couldn't be a pimple on a pimp's ass.*

The Original White Folks

Pimpin really ain't easy! Pimps are to hos what Accent' is to food, they wake up the flavor! Pimps and players are also said to possess magical powers and mystical sex appeal. Pimps are the only men on the planet that love, and are capable of understanding and dealing with hos based on who they are and what they do. When hos and lames (or any non-pimp) attempt to have a personal relationship, it's a prescription for disaster. That's like trying to mix oil and water. Tricks simply like the idea of having a ho, they don't really like the ho. Lame men will always harbor ill feelings for prostitutes, or ex-prostitutes. They will be distrustful, suspicious, jealous and some other shit. I can't understand how a professional hooker would want to be with anyone other than a professional pimp. The only advice a lame will offer is "I don't want you to do that any more," or "you need to get a real job." How much more real can you get than $200,000.00 + a year? However, that's why they are called lames. They don't know what this game is about... nor should they.

I understand to some degree, mostly because there are very few genuine prostitutes now days. Most of today's hookers and strippers are substitutes, wantstitutes or usedtitutes. This new breed of strippers and hookers have no pride in being in the game, they lack the class, style and knowledge to be good at what they do. The new hos are not in the game because they have any pride in, or respect for the game. Some of them don't even know or think they are in the game. **Therefore, it's impossible to be good at what you do when you don't know exactly what it is that you do.** "I ain't no ho, I'm an exotic dancer"

Selling pussy or stripping is just a quick or easy way for them to make money. These substitutes, wantstitutes and actors lack the common sense that pimpin and ho'in is a business and profession that requires skill and dedication.

The sheer nature of what hos do require the services of a pimp. All that a real ho needs to be and do cannot be accomplished without a pimp to guide, direct and assist her. It's a physical and mental impossibility for a ho to run the show and be the show at he same time. It's the same reason that every other successful professional in the entertainment industry, whether they are comics, rappers, actors, ballplayers, etc., have a manager, an agent, an accountant and a financial advisor. Big business cannot be accomplished without these services being performed. If it were not for having an agent/manager, Shaq would likely still be playing playground or alley ball at $100.00 per game. If you intend to grow and prosper, you need proper management, guidance, financial planning and direction.

The average lame only wants hos for what they do sexually. Pimps want hos because they are his **natural mate**; water seeking its own level. Pimps understand hos, and provide professional services hos can't do without. So, it boils down to whether a ho is a professional under proper instructions who gets top dollar, or a neighborhood tramp who gets a few bucks for hair-dos, nails and her cell phone bill. In other words, it depends on whether she is a ho or a ho-bo. I'm getting a little off the subject here, let me just say this: Certain things just go together, like:

Horse and carriage
Love and marriage

Shoes and clothes
Pimps and hoes

Every successful business or corporation has a CEO or a president, from McDonalds to the United States of America. One person runs the business, and that is NEVER the same person that does the work. Ronald Mc Donald **never** sells hamburgers. Neither one can be successful with out the other; it's a team effort. H&R Block cannot exist without taxpayers, and taxpayers won't get half of what they are due without H&R Block. Separately they won't make it, but together they make it "do what it do" for each other! I'm going to close with a few pimp slogans:

The Original White Folks

A ho without instruction
Is headed for self-destruction.

Big instruction brings about
big production.

If they knew better,
They would do better.

But they don't,
So they won't.

"There you have it. I only scratched the surface here, but I am sure you get the idea."   **--Folks**

Dear Player,

What is the difference between a pimp and a player?

-Monisha J., South Side, St. Louis

Dear Mo Jo,

All pimps are players, but all players are not pimps. I don't know what you've heard, but being a pimp only has ONE definition: a pimp accepts the earnings of a prostitute as a business or profession. In other words, if you are not checking money from a ho every day, you are not pimpin... point blank... no exceptions. One who pimps is playing the pimp game. However, players are not limited to one game; they may play any number of games including the pimp game. The following is a list of games a player may engage himself in. This list is by no means complete; it's just an attempt to make a point:

Check writing	*Illegal lottery &*
Identity theft	*Number Running*
Short & long con	*Boosting (Retail*
Pick pocketing	*store theft)*
Counterfeiting	*Shoplifting*
Murder Game	*Credit Card Scams*
Short Change	*Drug Dealing*
Con Artists	*Robbery/Burglary*

The Original White Folks

I gave a definition of what a player is and does a couple weeks ago, check your back issues. *Missing an issue of the Evening Whirl is still worse than missing a meal.* Last week I gave an explanation of why a ho needs a pimp. Thus, all that seems to be missing is an explanation of what a pimp is, or at least should be. Hopefully, this will round out the whole pimp and player question. I will provide a quote from my book, (Original Game):

"A PIMP is an ultimate gentleman; an impeccable dresser, well disciplined, knowledge-able, well manicured, sophisticated, and debonair... a charming smooth character who commands total respect. His vast knowledge and experience renders him capable of managing and directing the lives and finances of others. A pimp's mere presence should excite and electrify the average woman. At a bare minimum, the appearance of a pimp should peak any woman's curiosity and leave an unforgettable impact in her memory" [1]

The bottom line is that Pimps play the Pimp Game, and Players play all sorts of Game.

--Folks

---

[1]This definition is used as the opening line in Too Real for TV's film, Cross Country Pimping #3

Ask a player

Dear Player,

    I have been convicted of a misdemeanor, got probation and have satisfied all of my probation stipulations except paying the restitution. Now, the D.A. is saying that he is going to violate me and take my charge back to the felony it started off being. Can they do this? Is it legal?

-Rashieda H. 31, Chicago, IL

Dear Railroaded,

    No! It's not legal. Once the DA has allowed you to plead a felony down to a misdemeanor, it cannot revert back to the original felony unless you withdraw your plea or successfully appeal it. If you violate your probation for a misdemeanor, you can only be sentenced to a misdemeanor jail term. The DA cannot get a "second bite at the apple" simply because you are poor. Most judges will re-sentence you to community service in this situation. Our Constitution protects us against blatant violations of our rights to life, liberty and the pursuit of happiness. In particular, the 5th Amendment to the U.S. Constitution has a "*double jeopardy*" clause. What that means is that you cannot be twice placed in jeopardy for loss of life, liberty or property without due process of law. The situation you described violates both the 5th and the 14th Amendments to the Constitution. The 14th Amendment contains the "*due process*" clause.

In other words, you have had your day in court. You pled guilty to a misdemeanor, and that's all there is. Whatever the DA does, he has to do it with the misdemeanor; it's all he has to work with. The felony went out the window once he agreed to allow you to plead out, never to be seen or heard from again. So, either this DA is totally retarded, or he thinks you are and is using the felony, as a fear tactic, to get you to agree do something which is not in your best interest. That being said, I will close with the infamous words of Jessie Jackson:

"*May the Constitution go with you, the Bill of Rights protect you and may your own dreams be your only boundary henceforth, now and forever*"   **--Folks**

Dear Player,

I've always wanted to have sex with 2 men. Does that make me a nasty girl? How would I go about setting that up?

-D'Angela 27, Springfield, MO

Ask a player

Dear Praying for a Pair,

To answer your first question, no, you are not a nasty girl just because you have a fantasy you want to fulfill. Just as most men's fantasy is to have sex with 2 women, a number of women desire 2 men. The problem is that while men totally understand having their fantasy, they lack any understanding of a woman having a similar desire. Therefore, in answer to your second question, unless you have an extraordinary man, I would not suggest having him as one of your pair. You would do much better and have more success with a couple of guys who are friends or relatives. Two friends, brothers or cousins are more likely to be comfortable with each other. That works out to be much more fun for you. Friends and relatives will do more than strangers. They will be trying to out-do each other, which translates into more "do" for you.

Keep in mind that not many men will want to be naked in bed with another man, pussy notwithstanding. This also depends on the position you have in mind. One in each hole requires the guys to be closer than most men will be comfortable with. So, I would suggest you confine your desires to one in your face and one in the hole of your choosing, unless you can luck up on a couple of bisexuals. If you are too shy to approach 2 men with your double dick deal, you may want to recruit a friend with similar desires. The two of you can pull two guys into your fantasy and when you get where you're going, tell them you each want to double dip separately. This should give you more confidence and safety. Hell, you may just want to make it a 4-some and really get your freak on!

"There is nothing wrong with a little good clean fun between serious freaks. Use Condoms!"   **--Folks**

Dear Player,

How do I avoid the morning-after rhetoric with a woman I just met and just wanted to have a good time with?

-Just Want 2 Have Fun, 22, Da Lou

Dear Find em', fuck em' and forget em',

This does not take a brain surgeon to figure out. Get up and leave before she wakes up, or don't even go to sleep and leave when she passes out. In the event that you are in a hotel and wake up at the same time as your fuck buddy, tell her you left something in the car, go out and leave.

If you took her to your home, you get what you deserve. For the record, a nine-year old could have figured this out.

Just go!   **--Folks**

Dear Player,

My wife won't kiss me after I've gone down on her. What is that about?

-Roscoe D., South Side, St. Louis, MO

Dear Bass Master,

Maybe she is one of those, one in a thousand, women who doesn't like the smell or taste of fish. However, you can make one of a few choices here. You can do your kissing first and sucking afterwards, or give up one lick or the other. On the other hand, you shouldn't have a hard time finding a real freak that will kiss or lick anything or anyone and make it "do what it do."

Lick em' like you like em'   **--Folks**

The Original White Folks

Dear Player,

    I am a 22-year old college student. I am currently trying my hand at exotic dancing (stripping) to supplement my income. I am being over-run and overwhelmed by bisexual and lesbian dancers hitting on me and pimps trying to recruit me. I am not down with all of that, I just want to make some quick money. What's up with that?

-Allison Dillard, 22, St. Louis, MO

Dear Alice in Wonderland,

    When you fell through the looking glass, the first thing you should have realized was that you're not in Kansas anymore. It never ceases to amaze me how you squares and lames, with your spoon fed, plastic, contrived, middle class, white, American life-style and thought pattern, wander into the game and honestly believe the rules don't apply to you because you are not "in" the game, but are <u>only</u> doing this for a little while to get some quick money.

    Let me give you an analogy you can grab a hold to: *Driving a car:* It doesn't make a difference if you normally don't drive, or never drive and you are *only* driving a half block on a one time deal. If you are stopped by the police, you are subject to the same rules, laws and regulations as a professional driver who logs in a half million miles a year. You had better have a driver's license, registration, proof of insurance and an up to date license plate on the vehicle. You have to stop for red lights, yield at yield signs and drive on the right side of the street like everybody else, or you will be punished, (go to jail).

So, no matter whether you drive one inch or one million miles, if you are behind the wheel of a vehicle you are a driver, like it or not, and, therefore, subject to the rules of the road. When you pull out into traffic you have to blend in with the rest of the vehicles, get run over or maybe even killed. Again, it doesn't make one bit of difference whether you drive a half block or half way around the world. Get it? Ho up or blowup!

Ok, now we specifically deal with the fact that most strippers and or hookers are at least bisexual if not straight out gay. Strippers and hookers see, are presented with and requested to do (and do) something with dozens of dicks on a daily basis. Dicks are their job. This particular group of women tend to lose the average woman's fascination and desire for dicks to please them.

Adult entertainers see too many men, and dicks… Men that are totally shameless tricks and do a lot of sucker shit with their dicks. Hence, something they don't view as a job, and are not presented with on a regular basis, usually excites hookers and strippers: Pussy! You got that? Now about the "PimP problem", strip clubs and ho strolls are pimps' work places. These venues are where pimps work, recruit and make their living: They are on their job. The same is true of strippers and hookers.

So, with that in mind, how can you think, fathom or dream that you can enter Pimp's, stripper's and hooker's market place and life-style **with absolutely no** knowledge or training regarding where you are or what you need to do while you are there? Then, you have the unmitigated gall to complain! Additionally, you have the brazen audacity to be offended or put off because the people whose house you're in expect you to know and abide by their rules. You're visitor in someone else's home. You either act accordingly or leave!

Who do you think you are anyway, Princess Platinum Pussy? Buy a vowel you monkey-ass bitch! You are the one who is being tolerated here. You are in violation! You are taking food out of the mouths of people who do this for a living as a business or profession. And *you* don't like what *they're* doing? You need to see the wiz.

"*Either get in where you fit in, or get on before you're shit on!*"

"Go hard or go home." **--Folks**

Dear Player,

  Should I date someone who doesn't want to get an AIDS test?

-Tomiea 23, Tampa, Fl

Dear Dummy,

   The mere fact that you asked this question places your sanity at issue. However, despite the sheer insane nature of your having a second thought about playing with your life, I will supply you with an answer. Hell no! If this person's past sexual behavior has them in fear of the results of an AIDS test, you should be very afraid.

   "Run for your life!" **--Folks**

The Original White Folks

Dear Player,

I read your answer to why does a ho need a pimp and I must admit that I'm almost ready to choose. I still have second thoughts because of all the stories I've heard about pimps beating up their women, what's up with that?

-Quinesha Jones 21, Springfield, MO

Dear Ain't Down for Being Dunked,

I don't blame you. I wouldn't want to go anywhere I thought getting my ass whipped was a requirement either. An Atlanta cable television station recently interviewed me. In that interview, I was asked why pimps beat their hos. In turn, I asked the interviewer: "was your information about these alleged beatings obtained from either the pimps who performed these beatings or any of the alleged beaten hos?" She admitted that her question was based on what "they say… common knowledge"

That being said let me continue. I asked the interviewer if she watched the evening news on network television? She answered "yes." I asked, "if she was aware that nearly every week there was a story about a husband who killed his wife and/or her babies?" She replied "yes." I asked the same question related to boyfriends and got the same answer about the murder of girlfriends and their children. Then, I asked "if, in your entire life-time, you have seen a news report of a pimp killing a ho?" She thought long and hard and eventually answered with a quiet "no."

Finally, I asked: "Would it be safe for me to say, based on the news you've seen in your life-time, that a woman would be a hundred times safer with a pimp than she would with a husband or a boyfriend? (Common sense) She was speechless. If women really knew what charming smooth characters and ultimate gentlemen real pimps are, every woman would want one. There you have it. I commend you for asking your question of someone who actually has an answer based on fact, reality and personal experience. You have the makings of a real one. Good game!

"Don't cheat yourself-treat yourself."

Dear Player,

Can a woman be a pimp? I am pretty sure I could do it if I wanted to. I've got 2 women now who do what whatever I tell them.

Diane, Southside, St. Louis, Mo

The Original White Folks

Dear Diesel Diana,

Hell no! First and foremost a pimp is an *ultimate gentleman*. The important operative word here is *gentle* "man". No matter how many dildos you buy, how many baggy men's clothes you wear, or how many coochies you eat up or beat up, you are still a sheep in wolf's clothing. You can't think or act like a man, no matter how hard you try. You will always be a female, and you will have your monthly business to remind you of that on a regular. You can only act or think from a female perspective on how a man acts or thinks.

At any rate, it's all guesswork, smoke, mirrors, dildos and fantasy. Two women trying to be together as a couple is like the blind leading the blind. It's similar to Ray Charles leading Stevie Wonder through Madison Square Garden on fight night. They're not going to make it! They will be bumping into shit, crashing into people, stumbling and falling all over the place and won't get where they're going without guidance or direction.

If the average man can't do this PI thing, what makes you think a woman pretending to be a man can do it? Duh! Don't get it twisted here. I have no beef with your doing what you do. My problem is with you thinking you can or attempting to do what I do. Hey, if you like women, you like women, but you can't be the ultimate man. That's my job! You're *way* out of your league on that one babe.

"If it don't fit, don't force it."   **--Folks**

Dear Player,

   My sister Genieva is a dancer, (stripper). Genieva was recently indicted by the government for drug conspiracy. My sister never sold or possessed any drugs, but lived with a dealer. How can they charge her with a drug crime?
-Sabrina T., 31, St. Louis. MO

Dear Sister Sabrina,

   Unfortunately, this is an all too familiar story. I have personally known a number of strippers and hookers that have fallen victim to these same circumstances and received substantial federal sentences. A lot of young, inexperienced strippers/hoes are lured into playing girlfriend with dope boys. This group of players has astronomical amounts of cash they literally throw around. They offer to pay these girls' rent, buy cars, jewelry and designer sunglasses to wear at night in dark clubs.

Of course, these girls don't have the game or experience to realize that they are being set up off the rip. The reason the dope boys buy them cars is so they will have a delivery vehicle that's not in their name. The same is true of the apartment, which becomes "the stash spot".

Life becomes so good for these girls that they have little if any second thoughts about being the owner of the stash spot or even making a delivery or two. If they had $1/10^{th}$ of the game they think they have, they would know that using their home and telephone, as a distribution point for drugs is a serious felony. Bottom line: when the shit hits the fan, and it usually does because 75% of these "Players" or their friends are snitching, these girls are legally part of a drug conspiracy. The girls have dope and paraphernalia in their house and car. Thus, your sister is, according to federal law, part of an alleged drug conspiracy. The amount of the alleged drugs and her previous record will determine the length of the sentence in the event of a guilty verdict or plea… The Feds have a 98% conviction rate.

It's a sad affair that so many people, that are supposed to be slick, get themselves involved in so much sucker shit. It's the ills of the demise of the Original Game. Most young people these days get what they think is game off the stage instead of seeking the counsel of old school players.

Speaking of sad affairs, I have personally had strippers and hos tell me that they were "warned" not to talk to me because I have "too much game." I have a standard response to this statement, which is: "So, let me make sure I've got this right... you were "warned" not to talk to someone with game, right?" Just out of curiosity, who should you talk to, lames, tricks, other inexperienced strippers and hos, suckers? What would be the benefit in confining all of your conversations to lames? Learn to be more lame?" By George, I think you've got it! If you are following the lead of a lame what does that make you...a lamette? There is an old saying in the game:

IF YOU WALK WITH LAMES YOU WILL LIMP!!!

Now, relating this conversation to the current question, if your sister had been keeping the company or under instructions of a real player, she would have been seasoned with enough game and/or common sense to not allow tricks in the club, or anywhere else, to become boyfriends. **In the same way you can't turn a ho into a housewife, you can't turn a trick into a boyfriend or a husband.** If you're in the game and your man is a lame you are headed for disaster. What can he teach you, where will he lead you? What is the plan?

"A ho without instruction is headed for self-destruction"

--Folks

Dear Player,

I ran over my wife's ankle biting toy poodle and killed him. I never liked him anyway, but she has put up lost dog posters everywhere. Should I tell her?

-Luther B. Chicago, Ill

Dear Parent of a Missing Poodle,

Hopefully, you have enough game to have properly disposed of the corpus delecti. Let us also hope that you left no witnesses to the dastardly deed. Assuming that you discarded the problem pooch, I don't think it would be to your advantage to take the stand here. I would suggest you volunteer for poster duty and practice your lost best friend look. Actually, you never liked the "*little ankle biter*" anyway. So, this "accident" works to your advantage. I'm sure your wife's time was split between you and k-9 shorty.

Therefore, once poster duty proves to be fruitless and you properly play this off, you and Mrs. Poodle Pal can live happily ever after. It's been said that the truth will set you free. However, in this case, I believe that the truth will get you fucked up!

"Lie like a rug"   **--Folks**

Dear Player,

I think my wife is on drugs. Money keeps disappearing with nothing to show for it. Is there a way I can tell/see if she is?
-Amos Allen 44, Northside, St. Louis, MO

Dear Need to Know What the Biz Is,

The first thing I would suggest is that you ask her, she would know better than either of us. You may be right on point. However, you may very well be as far off base as black is from white. First of all, let me say that if you are half the man you think you are or claim to be, you would know your woman well enough to identify any change in her character and/or behavior. You would not need to ask me. That being said, if you have not noticed changes in your wife's behavior that would indicate drug use, maybe it's something else.

There are a few other possibilities that come to mind here. Did it occur to you that your wife may have a young pimp she's giving money to? She might have gambling habit, or maybe even a girlfriend? There is the possibility she's saving up to make a run for it. These are some of the most common causes of the problem you described. So, my suspicious friend, weigh all of the options and possibilities here and get back to me, ok?

"Investigate before you try to regulate" --**Folks**

Dear Player,

Is it important to "tell all" about my past to my new partner of about 9 months? At what point should I consider telling the truth?

- **Quintella S., 39 The Lou**

Dear Based on Bullshit,

From what I glean after a careful reading of your question, things seem to be working well for you as is. Therefore, if I were you, I would give due consideration to letting a sleeping dog lie. I don't see the advantage of growing a conscience at this late stage of the game. Let's not discount the fact that you have received less than the whole and nothing but the truth from your partner. This seems to be the perfect place to apply the old saying: "If it ain't broke, don't fix it." You should have laid the whole ugly truth out there off the break. Now that you've told a lie that your partner likes, it appears that in order to tell the truth you'll have to risk your relationship. So, you're going to have to make a big girl decision here. What do you value the most, your man or your conscience? Decisions, Decisions. That's your story and you're sticking to it. Good luck, because you are going to need it.

"Next time keep it real"   **--Folks**

Dear Player,

I just want to thank you for providing a forum for people to go to real life solutions that work. In today's age of information technology, it's still challenging at best finding a resource with genuine intelligence. I must admit that when I first saw your column I discounted it, deeming that there would be nothing of true value here. The word player and your big hat caused me to doubt your creditability, just like you probably will consider me some opinionated square bitch. Needless to say that not only was I wrong, but I was also pleasantly surprised to find your responses to be well thought out, witty and often times informative that apply to real life situations. Initially I thought you catered only to the "twenty something hip-hop subculture" of today's younger people. It is not only refreshing and entertaining to read your column, but reassuring to know that there is a reliable source of information for one to consult that is honest, has content of character, and a wealth of insight and wisdom. You prove your insight and wisdom to be invaluable especially in today's society.

While I am being forward, I must acknowledge the fact that my generation is directly responsible for the misguided youth of today because they are the end result of our parenting skills, or lack thereof which has molded them into who they are. Since they obviously aren't coming to us (their parents) for guidance and direction, it is good to know they have a platform where they can get accurate answers that also reflect on the consequences of their choices and actions. They seem unable to connect the dots between their thoughts in relation to how their lives are being lived. Failing to recognize that thought patterns influence lifestyles, choices and how they are living.

There seems to be such an appeal along with a propensity towards drugs and violence today. Everybody wants to be a player. Hopefully, they will avail themselves of the outlet you provide. They also have the added benefit of having access to 40 years of game without having to live through all the experiences. To learn from another's mistakes and reap the rewards of untold knowledge that spans from the streets to the courtrooms, you effortlessly transition from guns to gavel dispensing sound valid solutions, somehow bringing a sense of order where there once was pure chaos. Where we, the parents, have dropped the ball in our children's lives, you offer an alternative place for them to go with their questions. Proving age-old adages that are still true today, it takes a whole village to raise a child and our elders are to be revered and respected for their guidance, wisdom and direction.

When I read "why does a hoe need a pimp," I recognized we all need the same services. Your analogies are so profound because they show how hustlers and common folks both utilize the same organizational skills. All too often, our young people underestimate themselves. Feeling that they have no skills they can use in the real world. They don't realize that they have something to contribute to society. Not believing the skills needed to survive the streets to live past the age of twenty-five, with their life and freedom intact today is a major accomplishment. The game and life skills acquired can be transferred into big business. Plus, the fact is the same skills used to run an illegal operation are the same ones needed to operate a large corporation. In fact, one must have more knowledge, not only about what they are doing, but the law as well, in order to stay off the radar. Being able to pull that off in and of itself shows that one possesses the entrepreneurial spirit of which empires are made. Just like every deck of cards includes a joker, it will also have wild cards, trumps and the royalty of kings and queens. Who knows what lurks beneath the surface of these esteemed future leaders. I have a feeling that we have some real superstars in our midst. All that is needed is a plan to translate these skills to make a lateral move into the mainstream. The same way you have turned your 40 years in the game into a legitimate business. Walking your walk and talking your talk.

--Thanks, Yolanda 47, North Side, St. Louis

Dear Player,

My boyfriend of 2 years has proposed and I accepted. I used to be a prostitute and I am afraid to tell him. Should I?

-D'sire, 26, Atlanta

Dear Usedtitute,

I see at least 2 major problems with your situation off the rip. Now, other than the fact that you obviously bumped your head, let me expound. I'm sure you have heard the old saying that "you can't turn a ho into a housewife." However, in view of the fact that you're trying to turn yourself into a housewife, you get an exemption on that one.

The biggest problem here, the one that jumps out and screams for attention, is the absence of any real human emotion or passion. Let me explain. You and your boyfriend have agreed to spend the rest of your lives together; yet, you don't know a damned thing about each other! That's like signing a contract without reading it. This set of circumstances has become all too common. Your relationship is obviously built around sex instead of building the fucking around the relationship. In fact, you have no relationship! The only things you two have made a connection with are your sexual organs and the only thing you have exchanged is your bodily fluids.

There has obviously been no real exchange of information. Your relationship lacks the trust necessary to allow real, honest feelings and information to be exchanged. Thus, without having ALL of the information about each other's lives and thought patterns, true love and a lasting relationship are *impossible* to achieve. If your boyfriend likes the lie you've been telling him, it's the lie he wants to marry, not you! He doesn't even know you. So, if he likes booty, bullshit and blowjobs, how long do you think it will be before a bitch comes along with a fantastic lie, bigger butt and/or a better blowjob? If you're really serious about having a lasting, real, and honest relationship, it needs to be based upon something a lot more real and far reaching than booty and bullshit. Every woman has pussy. How many have honesty, realism and commitment? Try connecting mentally. This is supposed to be the "keep it real" generation, yet there are more fake moves and bullshit going on now than ever before in the history of *any* generation.

"Keep it real!   **--Folks**

Ask a player

Dear Player,

Is there any credence to the saying that people sleep around because they like "strange or different" from what they have at home? Sharissa, 27, Chicago

Dear Need Spice in your Life,

Yes! Variety is the spice of life! It is totally unrealistic, against human nature and beyond the average person's ability to control their libido to think that two people will fuck no one but each other for the rest of their lives. All you need for an answer to your own question is to relate sex to every other natural human activity you engage in. Ask yourself a few questions: Do you want to eat the same meal every time you get hungry, no matter how good it is? Do you want to wear the same outfit every time you get dressed, no matter how cute it is? I'm sure you are getting the point, so, I won't belabor the issue.

What separates the ducks from the geese here is the ability to be realistic and exercise plain ole common sense. There is nothing else in the human experience that is repeated the same way in the same manor with the same person or thing every time it's done. So, ask yourself, why are you unrealistic enough to think sex is an exception to the rule? The butt naked truth is that too much is made of the act of sexual intercourse. Think about it... two roaches can fuck. So, what is it really?

The biggest error committed by most people is that they attempt to build a relationship around sex.

Relationships should include sex, not be based upon it. See my answer in this column, to the "Usedtitute's" question, where I expand this train of thought. It applies directly to you. You are worried about the wrong thing. I suggest you spend your time wondering what your man does with his money instead of his dick. One, there is plenty of, the other there is never enough. Life is too short to spend any part of it worrying about something you can't do anything about anyway. What's really good?

"Follow the yellow brick road."   **--Folks**

Dear Player,

I'm at a crossroad. I was kicking it with a 23-year-old girl who I never expected anything from other than sex. I woke up out of my sleep one morning and realized I was in love with her.

The problem is that she has a girlfriend. I told her I was cool with that, do both. She says she has feelings for this other chick, but she cares about me. She's not sure what she wants to do.

-Get @ me. That nigga Wild, 29, Houston.

Dear My Girl got'a Girlfriend,

Bisexuality these days among young people, especially females, has become more of a fad than a sexual preference. Its almost expected behavior if you want to be "down." That being said, the first thing you need to determine is whether this girl is just experimenting or is a serious seafood lover. One way to find out if she's just fond of fish or totally in love with legs is to ask for an invite to the freak feast.

This way you can get a look into your girl's real feelings. Of course, her girl may not agree to an addition to the fuck and suck fest, but that is of little consequence. The important issue here is whether or not girlfriend is even willing to consider the move. It's also worthy of consideration that you have, or have not already been invited into her world of wild sex and unmitigated debauchery.

You need to know for sure if your girl is simply a freak and you have a chance at a relationship; or, if she has a serious love affair with Ms. Lickity split and you are just sideline entertainment. It sounds to me like girlfriend just likes to throw a party for her pussy every chance she gets. She sounds more like a tri-sexual. (She will try anything sexual.)

"Test the water before you jump in."   --**Folks**

Dear Player,

My sister is a high school dropout and has been "working the streets" for quite some time now. She has a nice house, a nice car and always has money. I went to college, am broke as hell and paying off student loans. I'm jealous but I don't understand how she can do this to herself. Please explain the life of a streetwalker.
-Mikala J., 27, Atlantic City, NJ

Dear Missed the Move,

First off, let me address your inability to "understand how she can do this to herself." It never ceases to amaze me how you squares and lames think, or I should say the way you don't think.

47

You have spent 4 years of your life working like a slave in school and spent untold thousands of dollars, which you still owe, and have no more than a bill to show for it. After all that, you discover that your less formally educated sister is doing much better than you.

You have actually convinced yourself that there is something wrong with what your sister is doing. Did it ever occur to you that you might have missed a step or two yourself? Maybe it's not what your sister is doing to herself but rather what you're not doing *for* yourself.

It sounds like your sister is taking full advantage of what she has to work with before it's too late. It also appears that your sister is using her money wisely. Buying a new home and car are indicators that she has good business savvy. Hopefully, your sister will invest in a legitimate business, which will allow her total benefit for the work she has put in. I suggest that you ask your sister about what she does and how she does it, instead of seeking advice and information elsewhere. I am of the opinion that you and sister girl have the makings of a very successful business team. You just have to get over your jealousy and stop hatin' long enough to smell the roses. This thought reminds me of the saying: *"Each one reach one and each one teach one."*

You have a serious "Rebecca of Sunnybrook Farms" attitude about what your sister does. However, if you took a long hard look at what you do it will surprise you.

I am willing to bet that all of the fucking you've ever done has been for free. You have met some guy at a club, thought he was cute or that he was a baller, left, went to a hotel and fucked like minks, sometimes with no condom. You have no doubt woke up alone in hotel rooms as well, only to eventually discover that the guy gave you an incorrect name and phone number.

Have you ever returned home at daybreak with your car out of gas, no cigarettes, if you smoke, still broke? Come on, you know you did. Be honest. After a night of marathon fucking and sucking seven ways to Sunday you end up dead broke, dead tired, with a sore pussy, hangover and empty purse. You honestly believe that shit makes sense? I would also be willing to bet that your sister gets paid well for any sex she has. I'll wager that she uses condoms for every act, including blowjobs. That's the way professionals get down. Personally, I can't understand how you do what you are doing to yourself. There is no glory in free-fucking, broke-hoing or whatever you lame ass bitches call it.

"You have a brain… use it in conjunction with your ass!"

--Folks

Dear Player,

I am from the south side of Chicago and I've seen pimps and players my whole life. I've always wanted to know why pimps and players all have more than one woman?

-KeKe, 24, Chicago

Dear Looking 2 Join?,

First off, let me explain, what pimps and players do is conducted as a business or profession. Now that we have that established, I shall proceed. Unlike the average man, pimps and players recognize that, most times and in many situations, the best man for the job is a woman. Thus, players and especially pimps entire business includes or is totally about women. Therefore, like any other corporation or business, pimps and players have a number of employees. The biggest difference between mainstream corporate business and what pimps and players do is that pimps and players have personal relationships with all their employees, whom are also their women. Therefore, the concept of "team effort" is increased tenfold.

Pimps and players are armed with the skills and ability to train women how to use their femininity and womanhood to the full extent. Most women don't realize the power they possess. A lot of the women that recognize their power, value and self-worth lack the knowledge of how to apply it to the average man, or the information regarding just how far a man will go for "the right woman." Then there is the fact that there is strength in numbers. So, the more people there are working toward a common goal, the more likely that goal is to be realized. Everyone involved can profit and learn from one another's strengths, weaknesses and skills. It's kind of like a hand picked family.

Imagine how well the family concept would work if you could pick your family members. The best thing about this kind of family is that anything you may need or want, sexually, emotionally, psychologically or materially, can be found within this type of family. It eliminates the need to ever have to let a stranger into your mix. That family is self-sufficient, safe, self-contained and totally efficient. Enough cannot be said for the incredible sexual fulfillment available. Under these circumstances, it is hard to have many, if any, problems as long as everyone is on the same page. However, in this day and age, it is hard to teach young women anything about game because they already know it all, at least they *think* they know it. At this juncture, I have gotten away from a direct answer to your question. Suffice to say that pimps and players have more than one woman in the same way that Microsoft or AT&T has more than one employee... Only more dedicated. If having one woman is a good thing, then having 10 women has got to be 10 times better!

"Team work makes the dream work."   --**Folks**

Dear Player,

I have gotten into some serious financial trouble. I need to make some dough quickly. What's the best way to flip some quick loot? You know $1 outta .15 cents.

-Larry D. Dogg, 21, Bensenville, Ill.

Dear Need a Quick Lick,

You can't put a square peg into a round hole. I would suggest you stick to what you know. The

American prison system is full of black men and women who needed some "quick loot." Don't be a statistic. If you are not a player, and do not posses specific knowledge and experience in making slick moves, don't do it! Stop and think for a minute. What would happen if you had never driven a car before, but needed to make a "quick trip" and decided to drive? Zapp! Bang! Crash! Kapow! Ok, now do you see the ills of fooling around with something you know nothing about or have never done before? You would be in the way of and endangering people who do know what they're doing. You would also be subject to getting yourself fucked up, really bad! That's why the game is so screwed up now because too many lames, that don't know what they're doing, are trying to be players.

"Don't get in where you don't fit in."   --**Folks**

Dear Player,

At 23 years old it has been hard for me to find a black man that has all the characteristics I am looking for. Believe me, I have looked; either they are too thugged out, gold teeth, saggy pants wearing fools, lame as hell, or they are on the down low. I love my black men. So, how can I find the right black man that is not too thugged out, stupid or gay? Where do I search?

Ask a player

-Alicia T, 23, Atlanta

Dear Looking for a Needle in a Haystack,

I believe you have the right idea about your search; you need to expand your perimeter. I am sure there are a number of young brothers who are neither thugged out, dressed in felony gear, sporting gold teeth, stupid, gay nor lame. However, you have eliminated a considerable portion of the young black males in your generation. If I understand your desires correctly, you are looking for a well dressed, educated or worldly, black heterosexual with game. With those requirements in mind, my first thought is of old school guys. The above description fits the average old school player to a tee. Of course, being an old school player myself, I couldn't resist the opportunity to get a plug in.

You really should, at least, consider raising the age limit for black men who comport with your requirements. You obviously have above average desires for your age and, thus, should consider older, above average men. You may need to make a big girl decision here. Another question that comes to mind here is: Wouldn't the average man, that fits your requirements, want to know what you are bringing to the table? You have quite a laundry list of requirements not to have listed any assets of your own. Let's stop and give due consideration here. Assuming you find Mr. Wonderful, ask yourself if you fit into his list of needs or desires in a woman? Obviously, the ideal man would have his own list of requirements for the woman of his dreams.

Therefore, I would suggest you evaluate your assets, values, possessions, goals and physical attributes. An honest review of your bag of goodies may produce the reason for the sad state of your current love life and prospects. You might need to get your weight up. In other words, the way you are living and thinking may be the reason you don't come in contact with the caliber of men you seek. Perhaps you need to upgrade your surroundings, associates, appearance and goals. I know nothing about you. Therefore, I can only generalize here. However, I believe most women can profit from this answer. If you haven't already done it, get your shit together! Look and think like the person you want to be or be with. Try hanging out at off campus clubs near upscale colleges, law schools and the like. Give the 30 something crowd a try.

Realistically, 20 something year olds are usually still searching for their goals and identity. You need to decide if you want to help someone grow, need help growing or want to grow with the man of your choice. There are a lot of us, both male and female, who desire unrealistic relationships. People in general need to get an honest handle on where they fit in, or what they need to do in order to fit in elsewhere.

"It's hard to soar like an eagle when you're surrounded by turkeys."   **--Folks**

Dear Player,

How do I approach a man I want to have sex with but says he won't wear a condom?

-Tammi T., 27, Burbank, Ca.

Dear Need to See the Wiz,

Approach him with all your clothes on from at least ten feet away, or not at all.

"If you play with fire you will get burned"

--Folks

Dear Player,

My wife won't give me head anymore. Before we got married she had no problem with

56

it, but now she doesn't want to do it. How can I get my wife to be the woman I married again?

-Luther D., 41, Kansas City, Kansas

Dear Looking for Loose Lips,

I will use one of my usual analogies to shed proper light on this situation. Your wife's behavior can be likened to that of a politician running for office. Your wife's blowjobs, before she became your wife, were like campaign promises. Once a politician is elected to office, the promises are rarely ever kept. Your wife, before she was your wife, was running for wife. She has been elected now and doesn't feel the need to continue the campaign blowjobs. Maybe, if she is made to feel like she is up for re-election the party may start up again. If you are not afraid, tell your wife that other candidates are running for the position. This maneuver will either bring out the best or worst in ole tight lips. One way or the other you can get the problem solved. Either your wife will get busy or get gone.

"Blow or go"   --Folks

Dear Player,

How do I let my man know that I want to explore sexually?

-Kiesha 34, Orlando, Fl.

Dear Sweet Polly Pure Bread,

Obviously, you haven't had much experience in the art of sex in the city. The fact that you are asking me this question tells me that your man doesn't have a large store of sexual moves either.

On the other hand, your man may have more moves than a master chess player and just wants you to remain Little Miss. Muffet. In either case, to answer your question, unless English is your man's second language, tell him what you want in plain English. I am 99% sure your man will comply with your requests. I want you to keep in mind that sexual exploration requires a lot of give and take on both sides. Third parties may come into play as well.

"Be careful what you wish for."   **--Folks**

The Original White Folks

Dear Player,

My friends and I were talking and came to the conclusion that a lot of men, over 30 years old dicks don't work. What happened? I thought one should get better with age. It seems to me they went into reverse then withered and died. Help!!!

-Monae, 25, Springfield, Ma

Dear Looking for a Stand up Guy,

First of all, let me state that I cannot be of assistance regarding your inability to find a "stiff one". However, I believe I can offer a reasonable explanation for the phenomenon you have described.

Ever since Viagra exploded on to the set, there has been as many, if not more, young men taking "the blue pill" than older guys. Viagra and a number of copy cat, generic versions of the drug were developed to cure "erectile dysfunction." This drug can create erections that last up to 4 hours for men who experience difficulty achieving an erection. Healthy young men with no problem getting it up began using/abusing Viagra to appear to be Godzilla in bed. The intended result was that these young guys wanted to become known among young women as "the best dick in town." For the most part, it worked.

However, your question and a number of other stories I've heard lead me to believe that permanent limp dick maybe a side effect of prolonged abuse of Viagra. We have to keep in mind that most of the sexually healthy abusers of Viagra also partake of alcohol, Ecstasy, Cocaine, marijuana or all of the above.

The mixture of these drugs has the potential to create incomprehensible side effects and long term medical malfunctions. I have always been of the opinion and expressed it regularly that if you are taking Viagra to help with your dick at 20 something years old, what the hell are you going to need at 40? Maybe a Viagra pill the size of an elephant?

There are no tests to support my theory and the results are not in on the tests that have been done. However, common sense should provide some guidance here. Trust me, reaching the age of 30 is not normally a dick death sentence. There is much more at work here. Hell, I'm 60 years old and with absolutely no help, my "Johnson" will rise to the occasion at the drop of an ass. Additionally, I have had no complaints from either 20 something through 40 something year old women regarding my performance, technique or longevity. I still make it **do** what it **do** on sheer animal sex drive and god given talent.

"If it ain't broke don't fix it."--**Folks**

Dear Player,

I have hung out in a bar where pimps and Player's hang. I've heard the term "bottom bitch" a lot, but never quite got the real meaning of it. Can you explain?

-David H., 26, Charlotte, NC

Dear Got No Shame Seeking Game,

Pimps that have a number of hos use the term "bottom bitch" most frequently. A bottom bitch is usually the ho that's been with him the longest and, therefore, knows exactly how he wants things done. Although, the bottom bitch doesn't necessarily have to be the one who has been there the longest. More often "the bottom" is the one who has the most game and leadership ability, no matter when she arrived. She's the best man for the job so to speak. Now that we have that established, we can continue on to the duties of a bottom bitch. In layman's terms, a bottom bitch has superior knowledge of the game and the man she's with. Thus, she manages the rest of the girls on the team.

The bottom bitch performs all of the duties that do not require the immediate attention or action of a pimp. She functions as a pimp's personal assistant and makes sure that the rest of the girls' wardrobe; hair and nails are up to par. She makes travel arrangements, monitors web sites, makes appointments, provides transportation and arranges bail bonds and legal fees. She makes sure the overall day-to-day operation of the business is properly handled. A bottom bitch has the ability and authority to run the show in a pimp's absence. As in any other business, the manager (bottom bitch) can and does run the entire operation. This allows a pimp the freedom to pursue other ventures and the opportunity to travel.

So, in conclusion, a bottom bitch is that bad bitch that totally handles a pimp's business from A to Z. She's something like a madam; something like a pimp. She's the head bitch in charge (HBIC), but always a ho that recognizes the true value and worth of being down with a professional gentleman of leisure. She is the ultimate man's ultimate woman, his mate, his lover and partner.
**"A bottom bitch is a bad, bad bitch!"
Folks**

The Original White Folks

Dear Player,

How can I keep my man/relationship fresh/interesting through the years?

-Ruby, 35, St. Louis

Dear Want to Keep it Romantic Ruby,

As I have answered so many times before, having threesomes with another woman and your man is one of the slickest moves a woman can make. Of course, you have to have total confidence in yourself and your man. You need to really know that having a threesome is entertainment for the evening. It's kind of like a live performance, when the show is over everyone goes home happy, fulfilled and it's over. If you are insecure in yourself or your relationship, this is not the move for you. Trust is a key issue here. A threesome can be the most fun you've ever had or your worst nightmare, depending on your level realness and how much freak you have in you. Talk about it at length. You don't want any surprises.

Start off slow. Have a plan of what you want to do and don't want to do. Talk to your third party and make sure she knows the plan or that there is no plan and anything goes. Also, there are a number of toys and sexual aids available at adult stores: Vibrators, vibrating butt plugs, two-headed dildos for two women or threesomes, heat generating motion lotion and flavored lubricants. You will discover a whole new universe of sexual pleasure if you investigate these wonderful toys.

"Find out what's really good"   **--Folks**

Dear Player,

I find myself back on the market after terminating a long-term relationship. I feel like I'm in a foreign country. What do I do or how do I go about dating?

-Tia, 43, Baltimore, Md.

Dear Don't Know How to Date,

Very carefully, you need to re-educate yourself on the new rules. I don't know how long you've been "off the market," but it sounds like you are in for a rude awakening. To some extent, it appears that you are aware of the new set of circumstances you have to consider when picking a man. These days you have to consider drug abuse, Herpes, HIV, AIDS, HPV, men being on the "down low" and a host of other things you probably didn't have on the table before. Having a good job, being a loving, caring person or having children by a previous "baby mama" has been placed at the bottom of the list of things to be weighed when currently shopping for a man.

"Get a good look before you leap because the life you save may be your own."   **--Folks**

Dear Player,

I'm dating a woman who is frigid, what do I do?

-Delbert B., 31, Southfield, MI

Dear Need to Turn a Geek into a Freak,

The first thing I suggest you do is identify the source of Icebox Slim's frigidity. There is something in her background or childhood that inhibits her ability to even want to enjoy sex. Maybe this woman was the victim of sexual molestation as a child, or a rape victim later in life. These are some of the most common reasons for the syndrome you describe. So, you first have to identify, and then deal with the reason for your woman's inability to "do the do." You have to convince her that sex is her friend because at some point in her life sex was a source of discomfort or pain for her.

This will not be an easy or quick process. Take your time and be gentle. If this is done properly, you may end up with a world-class freak. Once this woman gets past whatever is holding her back, she may try to make up for lost time. A trip to the adult toy and video store will also prove helpful in your endeavor to loosen ole girl's butt cheeks. Show her what other women do and how much fun they have doing it.

"Pussy is a terrible thing to waste."   **--Folks**

Dear Player,

How do I ask my mate about her past sexual relationships without offending her?

-Ulman Beecher, 46, St. Louis

Dear Wanna Know about the Ho,

Actually, in a real relationship, you shouldn't have to ask. Obviously, you are in a less than ideal relationship. Two people that have decided to share each other's lives and don't share their past experiences or relationships are headed for disaster. I hear his stuff all the time but still cannot understand what you people base your relationships on? It's certainly not on honesty, realism, trust or a true sense of togetherness. Yours is no doubt one of those relationships based purely on sex. After having sex, you try to build a relationship around the fact that you fucked.

A real relationship should include fucking but not be based on it. The actual act of having sex takes a few minutes, an hour if you're lucky and no more than 4 hours with Viagra, that's if you're 20 years old. What you do with the other 20 to 23 ½ hours in a day is the issue? Do you have anything else in common? Damnit man, use some elementary thought here.

However, to answer your question, don't worry about offending her, just ask.

"Look under the hood before you buy a car."

--Folks

Dear Player,

How do I get my woman to fulfill my fantasy of sleeping with 2 women?

-Freddie Johnson, 24, Springfield, Ma

Dear Freaky Freddie,

Most women either already have, or at least seriously thought about having sex with another woman. Having a man involved keeps it legitimate and makes it a freak move instead of a lesbian act.

So, if you are as smooth as you think you are, it shouldn't be hard to talk your woman into trying this activity. I honestly don't think it will take a lot of convincing. For the most part, you will be providing an outlet for something she has always been curious about, (or just has not told you about). Also, see my answer in this column to Romantic Ruby's question

"Make it do what do with two"   **--Folks**

Dear Player,

Do pimps and players ever think about getting married and settling down? Don't pimps and players want love too?

-Shariffic, 24, Gary, In.

The Original White Folks

Dear Wanna Marry Myself a Pimp,

Pimps and players live and operate outside of the box. Therefore, the way average lames live or conduct their business is not the way of a pimp or a player. I don't need to go to a church I normally don't go to, in front of a preacher I don't know, and tell my woman, in front of our family and all of our friends that she is my woman. Hell, she already knows that. Notwithstanding the fact that the institution of marriage requires both parties to tell each other a bold face lie. i.e. You are required, in a marriage ceremony, to promise to fuck no one but each other for the rest of your lives... blah, blah.

Pimps and players operate on a much higher plane and more realistic level than your average John Q. Citizen. Thus, true pimps and players recognize that the whole idea upon which getting married is based is a cruel joke. That's why at least 65% of all marriages end in divorce and the other 35% have on-going outside relationships. It's totally unrealistic. Marriage is based upon middle-class American standards. If you are not middle-class and/or American, that shit doesn't apply to you.

However, back to your question, the only real "benefit" of marriage is to:

Ask a player

1. Give children the father's last name.

2. Insure that money and other property is fairly distributed in the event of a break up or death.

Long-term relationships that players, pimps, hos and other women in the game engage in have the same degree of legality without all the bullshit. Anyone affiliated with real game has enough common sense to make sure they get their just due out of the deal. Pimps and players have lawyers who make sure everything is done according to law. Women, who are or have been in long-term relationships with real pimps and players, end up with homes, businesses and a stock portfolio. Herein lies the difference between the genuine article and commercialized lames and suckers. There is a level of togetherness and commitment between people in the game that is rarely achieved or understood by anyone else, especially lames. A pimp or player knows that if his woman has sex with another man it's because she's going to get paid and will use condoms. And, of course, that money goes to the betterment of both of their lives. Lame women, house wives & girlfriends, sneak and fuck for the fun of it and risk STD's, AIDS, HPV and possible death using no protection in the process. Wow!

The Original White Folks

By the same token, women in the game know, without question, if their man has or is with another woman it's because she is giving him money or providing some valuable service. (Not a blow-job) It's a known fact that she is on the team and is bringing more than her ass to the table. House-husbands and boyfriends trick off a hundred miles an hour in a 25mph zone. They have been known to trick off the rent, food and bill money for a shot of ass from a perfect stranger that wouldn't even speak to him were it not for money. I'm sure I've made my point here.

To give a direct answer to your question, pimps and players have a higher level of understanding with their women than marriage could ever reach. As for love, how can a man not love a woman who does everything she can to make their lives better? That's realness to the 10th power. Pimps and players don't consummate their relationships in the same manor as girlfriends, boyfriends or husbands and wives.

"Never mind getting married, try getting an understanding that works."

--Folks

Ask a player

Dear Player,

I'm in love with a man who doesn't have any money, motivation, goals or desires. I have to push him to do anything. I want to leave but just the thought of not being with him hurts.

-Heather, 27, Las Vegas

Dear Boyfriend's Get Up and Go Got Up and Went without Him,

First of all, I want to point out the fact that your boyfriend's behavior didn't recently start. Your man's attitude has been with him all of the time. Therefore, its obvious that the source of your current complaints were present off the rip, but you over looked all the bullshit in pursuit of sex and "a man." You were dazzled by the dick and therefore blind to the bullshit attached to it. A significant number of women, especially the lonely, in their desire for sex and "a man," experience this same blindness. Some never see the light. Fortunately, you have the wherewithal to finally take a realistic look at your boyfriend and see past the sex and companionship.

I talk about these types of relationships all of the time. Enough cannot be said for having a

72

relationship first and building the sex around the wonderful mental connection you have made. More and more I see and hear about these, so-called, relationships based purely on blowjobs, booty and bullshit, instead of understanding, reality and common sense. Once one of these "feel good" relationships gets started, women become caught up in their feelings and the comfort of not being alone. These women fail to see that they are going nowhere other than the bedroom. The bottom line here is that you should, with no hesitation, get away from anyone who cannot take, or at least lead you into a better life. Try finding a thinker first and a good fuck later. Human dildos are found anywhere.

Think about it, you are no further ahead than you were before sweet daddy good dick came along. In fact, you are most likely behind. You have to feed, sleep and clothe two grown people instead of one. The time and effort you have put in dealing with this lame could have been channeled into upgrading your life style, continuing your education, perhaps a new business venture, job, etc.

Notwithstanding the fact that **if** the *right man* came along, he would by-pass you because you have this human dildo hanging around your neck. Get rid of the dead weight and step your game up. You have a brain. Let it take you past your ass and heart and lead you into a better life. Make sure your brain is engaged before putting your ass in gear.

"If you change your mind your ass will follow."

--Folks

Dear Player,

Should I be concerned that my husband has started spending more time at the office than usual?
-Cynthia Gibson, 37, Milwaukee

Dear Worried about the Wrong Thing,

If I understand your question correctly, you are asking if you should be concerned that your husband may be getting a *Lewinski* at the office. If that is the case, your thoughts are misguided to say the least. Your hubby getting head at the office means less work for you at home. As I have stated many times before, you should be worried if extra time spent at the office translates into less money. Now, if your husband's paycheck reflects the extended hours spent at the office, what exactly is your beef? You cannot regulate his "Johnson" nor can you measure the mileage on it. The only thing you can do here is create a lot of stress and mental anguish for yourself and your man about something you can do nothing about anyway. Your concern and effort would be better spent making sure your man has and uses condoms. Now that's something genuinely worthy of concern. It's literally a matter of life and death. Try keeping up with the money

"You can't miss what you can't measure."
--Folks

Dear Player,

My man is addicted to porn- what should I do?
-Louise Williams, 26, Kansas City, Mo.

Dear Need to Get Your Freak Up,

I answered a similar question a while back for a woman whose man was addicted to strip clubs. So, I will give you the same answer I gave her, as it applies the same for both situations. If you do the kind of stuff he watches he won't have to watch porn. I have a move that's guaranteed to work. The first thing you have to do is get rid of your little Miss Muffet, high school girl, preacher's daughter ideas about men, sex and relationships. Get Real! Your man is a freak! He can't resist a big butt and a smile. Men watch porn for a number of reasons. I will not attempt to list them all. However, I can reduce them down to the lowest common denominator:

1. Man's natural instinct is sexual.

2. The desire for variety in the male sexual experience is as common for a man having a "Johnson".
3. 98% of all men are total idiots when it comes to women and sex.

Porn offers a variety of butt, boob and body sizes. This assortment, along with the fantasy atmosphere, is usually the drawing card.

You want to keep your man away from porn, have a threesome. Invite a sexy female over for fun and games. This activity will allow your man to keep his money, get the variety he desires and do it live. In turn, you both will enjoy better sex and a better relationship. Your man will actually love and appreciate you MORE because you will have proven that you are one of those, "one in a thousand," women who can appreciate the real. Last, but not least, you and your sexy friend can get your freak on all in the name of pleasing your man. At some point you should disregard what *should be* or what is *supposed to be* and deal directly with what *IS!*

"If you can't lick em, join em."　　　　**--Folks**

Dear Player,

I have a friend who is considered to be a thoroughbred player. He has been giving me game that has worked. I have profited from his game. However, I understand that game ain't free and I pay my dues when they are due. However, people hate on that. I am told that I shouldn't give him money. What should I do and why do people hate like this?

-Taneesha (always hated on) 26, New York, NY

Dear Hated On,

I feel your pain sista. There are very few people these days that have reached the level of truth, realism, understanding and game, which you seem to have achieved. Almost everybody is on some form of fake, unrealistic, lame bullshit. It's refreshing to know that someone as young as yourself has a realistic handle on both life and Game as well. Most people, especially your generation, has no clue about real life, much less real game. They are hypnotized by rappers, the music and designer names and honestly think that shit is game

As I have pointed out so many times in my books and in this column, real game is passed down from one generation of players to the next. If you're not getting your game from an old school player, you're not getting game... you are getting bullshit! Your friend's lack the game or understanding of real life prevents them from having the heart or confidence in themselves to seek it. Therefore, they find it more convenient to hate on game, rather than seek it out. These kinds of people are so game conscious and afraid they are going to be played that they end up playing themselves. They're actually running from what's real. The problem is that there are so many of them. They get together in groups, and attempt to justify the poor excuse for a life they live and the lame ass shit they do by hating on real players. They don't have the mental capability or the realness to wrap their pea brains around the concept and participate. Instead, they convince themselves and try to lead others to believe that there is something wrong with what's real and actually works.

You need to stay strong, believe only half of what you see and none of what you hear. Continue to make the supreme effort and seek real game. Don't let anyone, bitch, bulldog or baby sway you from the path of righteousness and the pursuit of the real. Having real game is equivalent to being a mental multi-millionaire, and, like being a financial millionaire, very few people ever achieve that status. They don't have what it takes. [Real Game]

This is why 95% of the world's money is owned by 5% of the world's population. The other 95% of the people in the world are scrambling trying to get a piece of the other 5% of the money that's left out there. See what I mean? Yeah!

Back to your question about giving money to a player who gave you the game to get it in the first place: That concept shouldn't be rocket science. I can't imagine someone thinking they shouldn't share money with a person that made it possible for them to get it. There would be no money at all if it were not for the assistance, guidance and direction from this player. "Game is to be sold not told." You should consider yourself blessed to even know a thoroughbred player, much less have one actually share real game with you. The real beauty of a player giving you game is that he can't take it back. Once you've got it, it's yours to use for life. So, why not give him a genuine token of appreciation for something you will use for the rest of your life? Even if you don't give this player money based on the realness of the situation, you need to provide him a reason to give you more game. More game translates into more money and you know how the rest of it goes... It never ceases to astound me how utterly stupid lames and their thought patterns can be. Not showing love to someone that puts money in your pocket is like burning down your own home. Where will you go then? What can they be thinking? Well, obviously, they're not thinking.

You keep doing what you're doing girlfriend. Keep that thoroughbred as close to you as you keep your money. He is capable of upgrading your game to his status if you have the game and common sense to allow him. Obviously he's already decided to give it to you. Don't fuck up your blessing and more importantly, don't let anybody else fuck it up.

"If you walk with lames you will limp!"   --Folks

Dear Player,

I was arrested for a DUI. When I first got pulled over, I passed the field test. I counted, blew in the gizmo, walked the line and touched my nose. The officer decided to take me in

anyway. The cop said he smelled alcohol and wanted a urine/blood test. I took it. They said I failed. I was over the limit. I was arrested and jailed. When I went to court, I discovered they lost both the samples and the test results. The DA wants me to plead guilty. The DA said he knows and I know I'm guilty. What should I do?

-Glennice H., 31, Cleveland, Oh

Dear To Be or Not to Be,

Our American system of justice requires the government to **prove** the guilt of an accused person before one can be convicted. In criminal cases, the standard of proof is *beyond a reasonable doubt.* In a civil matter, the standard of proof is less stringent. Civil suits or civil infractions, such as a traffic offense, require proof based upon a *preponderance of the evidence*, which means that at least 51% of the evidence has to be against you in order to convict you of an infraction or prove you liable for damages in a lawsuit.

The important operative word here is **proof**. The only exception to the requirement of proof is if an accused person pleads guilty or admits responsibility in a lawsuit. Thus, if you don't tell on yourself, the moving party, the DA or person bringing a lawsuit, has to offer proof to the court. If there is no proof, it is a legal impossibility for one to be convicted of anything.

In your case, the proof of driving under the influence is the toxicology report from a lab. Without the report there is no case unless, of course, the DA can convince you to convict yourself. The DA's office will take a conviction any way they can get one. I hope you're not trying as hard to convict yourself as they are?

All you have to do at this point is plead not guilty and justice will take it's course from there. The DA himself will move to dismiss the charge because if there is no proof, therefore, no case. The DA will not want to make himself look stupid, although he obviously had no difficulty asking you to do something as stupid as convicting yourself in a case that has no evidence.

"You have a Constitutional right to remain silent… Use it!"   **--Folks**

Dear Player,

My sister says I'm nasty because I have threesomes with my man and other women. Yet she changes guys like I change socks. How do I

respond to her? What can I say to shut her mouth?
-Special T., 31, Atlanta

Dear Sister of Can't Get Right,

The first thing that is obvious here, other than the usual sibling rivalry, is that your sister is both sexually frustrated and unable to adequately deal with men. Let me explain. On one hand, you are comfortable with your sexuality, your relationship and sense of reality. Your ability to not only keep your man, explore sexually with him and another woman, all the while maintaining a healthy state of mind shows that you are a well-rounded woman. On the other hand, your sister is severely psychologically and sexually bankrupt.

All women have at least thought about sex with another woman. However, most lack a sense of reality about being a freak and live their entire lives in denial and sexual frustration.

Your sister's frequent changing of men is indicative of an unhealthy state of mind. The inability of a woman to keep a man any length of time is evidence of sexual inexperience and frustration as well as psychological and emotional bankruptcy. In other words, she probably has bad sex, no imagination, expects unreasonable and unrealistic things from men and is a pain in the ass! In your sister's frustration, she has to convince herself that there is something wrong with what/how you do, in order to justify her own shortcomings. (No pun intended.)

You have a good relationship. Both you and your man get your freak on, keep it real and enjoy a happy and fulfilling relationship. Sister girl just hates because she can't get it right. Let's hope that she requires her constant entourage of men to use condoms. Your sister has too many portions and not enough passion.

"Right is no better than wrong if it doesn't work."

--Folks

Dear Player,

We seem to have a lot of rats in our operation that seem to be cutting deals with the police. What are some of the signs that you have a traitor in your camp?

-Memphis Mouse, 28, St. Louis

The Original White Folks

Dear Looking for a Weak Link,

I cannot properly answer your question, mainly because I have no experience or knowledge about snitches to draw from. Just on common sense, I would say that if you are experiencing an unusual number of busts, someone is talking. A chain is only as strong as its weakest link. Look for yours.
I go out of my way to surround myself with people who are proven thoroughbreds.

I've checked their pedigrees or know for a fact how they function under pressure. Other than that bit of advice, unfortunately, I can't offer you much else. Keep lames out of your life.

"Stay sucker free"   --**Folks**

Dear Player,

I have sex with a lot of strange men when I get drunk. I used to think that drinking too much made my pussy hurt, but now I realize it's my behavior not the liquor. I'm OK with the sex part. I just don't over-do it now. So, does this mean I can hold my liquor?

-Johnny Mae, 39, Waycross, Ga.

Ask a player

Dear Find'em, Fuck'em and Drink up Their Shit,

No! That does not mean you can hold your liquor. What it means is that you are a drunken slut who is sick and tired of her pussy waking up with a black eye! If you are having marathon fuck fests with multiple total strangers while in a drunken stupor, you don't even know who these people are, how many there are or if they used condoms? You are worrying about the wrong thing here. Having your pussy pulverized should be the least of your concerns. You need to be tested for HIV/AIDS and all other STDs. Moreover, you need mental and substance abuse counseling. Last, but certainly not least, you need to see the Wiz and get a brain before you fall through your own dumb ass and break your free fucking neck!

"Step back and take a realistic look at yourself. I promise, you will not like what you see"   --**Folks**

Dear Player,

What, if any, difference is there between a porn star and a prostitute?

-Tammie, Atlanta-South Side

The Original White Folks

Dear Wanna Know About a Different type Ho,

Oh, there is a gigantic difference on several fronts. First and foremost, the biggest difference is that, unlike genuine prostitutes, porn hos lack realism. This absence of reality applies directly to the porn participant's unrealistic perception of themselves and what they do. They have no idea who they are or what it is they really do. First off, let me point out that every fuck film participant I've ever spoken with has referred to herself as a "porn star," "exotic film star" or some variation of those terms... always ending with the word "star." These women have the illusion that they are some type of movie star simply because they have eaten a coochie or done a blow job while shoving a 14 inch dick up their ass in front of a movie camera. There are actually some real *porn stars* in the industry who get the big bucks for what they do. However, they come few and far between. [No pun intended.]

Most female porn participants only get a few hundred bucks and/or the world renowned film producer's promise: *"I'm gonna make you famous!"* or *"You're going to be a star!"* Thus, there are a number of these "star" wannabes who actually "work" for free in pursuit of an illustrious, grand exalted "porn star" career. These women, in their attempt to defraud themselves into believing they are not prostitutes, engage in 5 to 10 times more sexual acts, for the same money, a genuine ho would charge for any one of those acts. So called "porn stars" will perform any and every sex act known to mankind seven ways to Sunday, and on most occasions, it's done for short money. Sometimes even small farm animals get into the act. That being said, a large number of these women have actually fooled themselves into thinking the fuck film industry is not prostitution. A look at the New Expanded Webster's Dictionary definition of prostitute and prostitution will prove very helpful here:

> Prostitute: *"to offer publicly for lewd purposes for hire; openly devoted to lewdness; a female given to indiscriminate lewdness."*

> Prostitution: *"practice of offering the body to indiscriminate intercourse with men; debasement."*

These definitions cover both out-right ho'in and XXX film participants alike. Therefore, the difference between hos and "porn hos" is how much "work" each puts in for same amount of money. So, either you know you're a ho **or** you do the blow for short dough... and call yourself a star on the go. This sad state of affairs is yet another example of how the last two or three generations have been hoodwinked, bamboozled and led astray by movies, the music and a lack of true game or recognition thereof. In this day and age, the commercialized, fake version of most things is more acceptable than the real. **It's impossible to be good at what you do if you don't really know what it is you do.**

Unfortunately, porn pussies, strippers and the like are some of the hos who lack the common sense or general knowledge that they are hos; in turn, they fuck up the game trying not to be who or what they really are. The level of sheer stupidity in today's adult entertainment industry is scary. There was a time when prostitutes were some of the slickest women on the planet.

These days most hookers, strippers and "exotic film stars" are as dumb as a bag of rocks. What porn hos do is paid for once and sold by someone other than the ho for years on end. They get fucked coming and going. The film producers get millions. If one of these "film stars" asks a producer to help them out of a tight financial situation, they will most likely be thrown out or invited to a dick for their troubles. On the other hand, a genuine prostitute will have gotten enough money for what she does or have enough game not to have to ask anyone for anything, at any time.

What real prostitutes do is paid for once, done once and she's the one who gets paid for the act. If the person paying likes what has been done, and wants to see or do it again, they will have to pay her again and again and you know how the rest of it goes... There is no rewind button. Unfortunately, from a technical standpoint, I have to label both porn movie participants and strippers as hos. (Although that's a slap in the face to genuine hos.) This "other" group of hos are not very good hos. They are cheap hos, but hos nonetheless!
"If they knew better they would do better, but they don't, so they won't."   **--Folks**

Dear Player,

    I'm at the end of a 30-month sentence for the feds. Before I got busted my girl was with me every day. She didn't have to do nothing. I bought her a car, jewelry, clothes, the whole 9, anything she wanted. So, tell me why my girl got with my friend as soon as I came to prison? Now, she wants to get back with me when I get out. –

Big D, 31, Lockdown, Miami, Fl

The Original White Folks

Dear Your Girl got a Boyfriend,

Let's take a look at this situation from a purely academic standpoint. When you and your girl were together and you were rolling, what did you teach her? I am willing to bet my left nut that you didn't teach girlfriend how to hustle. You would have had a sucker stroke and been willing to murder her if you even thought or dreamed she sold pussy or worked in a strip club. You didn't send her to college or a technical school. I'm also willing to wager that you told girlfriend she didn't have to do anything because you made enough money for the both of you, right? Yeah, I know. So, in essence, the only thing you taught her was to lay up under a man who is balling, and freak with him. Those were the only requirements she had to fulfill and all of her dreams would come true. Well, my brother, she is doing *exactly* what you taught her to do, i.e., get under a baller and freak for whatever she needs.

Again, from an academic point of view, your woman deserves big ups. Not many women do *exactly* what they've been taught by their man. The down side to this deal is that you didn't teach her anything other than sucker shit. It's like money in a bank. You can only get out what you put in. So, when you get out, I suggest you take her back. This time teach her something real and keep your dick in your pocket. Girlfriend seems to follow orders well. Give her some game, *if you have any*, and you will have a world-class woman. Hopefully, you will allow both your incarceration and the situation with your girl to be a serious life lesson. This is education at its best. Use it to your advantage. Girlfriend wants to be with you, she just did what you taught her while you were gone. If there is anyone to blame here, it's **you!**

"The best way to get on your feet is to get off your ass"   **--Folks**

Dear Player,

   I got a little game and I want more. I left my lame ass boyfriend and called myself getting with a Player. I found out that even though my present boyfriend hustles for a living he's just as big of a lame and tricks off his money just like the 9 to 5 lame I left. What's up with that? Forget soldier, I need game. I need a Player!

-Rohneeta, 23, Dallas, Tx

The Original White Folks

Dear Got a Pinch but Need a Pile,

You are a victim of your generation. It's not really your fault. Part of the problem, as I have pointed out numerous times, is the misuse and abuse of the words pimp and player. Almost no one in your generation seems to know the real meaning of those words. Therefore, you don't have much of a yardstick by which to measure the meanings. Then, there is the common practice of men, especially the younger ones, tricking off their money. This mass tricking is brought on, in no small part, by the music and videos. **Make it rain!** Of course, what the average person fails to realize is after those video shoots are over, the rappers pick all of their money up and put it back in the bank.

I wouldn't feel bad about not being able to locate a player right off the rip. Keep in mind that 98% of all men are total suckers and tricks when it comes to women and sex. Thus, you are looking for a needle in a haystack. The way people throw around words like player and pimp these days makes finding the genuine article extremely difficult. Everybody claims to be a pimp or a player. A good rule of thumb is to disregard what people say and watch what they do. The last couple generations have produced some serious misconceptions and misdirection about game, players and pimps. Don't get this twisted, there are some real ones… you just have to look closely.

"When you absolutely, positively have to have a bona-fide answer… **ASK A PLAYER!** " **--Folks**

Pimps and Players do not make it rain… they make it drain! **--Folks**

Dear Player,

At what point does a couple, two people, move from "just fucking" each other to having a relationship? Is there a time frame for this stuff?

-**Donethia, 26, Boston, Ma.**

Dear Don't Blow Your Blessing, (No pun intended)

Don't make your move too soon. There is an age-old game rule that comes to mind here; sometimes the best game in the world is no game at all. In your case, the best relationship you can have may very well be no relationship at all. Let me explain. Some of the best deals two people can have with each other is sex. They have nothing else in common, but totally and completely enjoy one another sexually. Thus, if these people attempt to do anything other than fuck, it more than likely will be a fuck-up. So, you may be in the process of ruining a good thing. In direct answer to your question, no, there is no time frame in which to switch from fucking to playing house. For the record, I know that a couple is two people. I don't have enough information to make an accurate determination here. However, it doesn't sound like you and your fuck buddy do much else together. There are a number of factors to be considered to begin a relationship. Do you go out socially? Have the same hobbies? Do you work in similar fields? Have children? Want any? Share the same friends? Can you help each other get where you are going in life? Or, does he just have good dick? See what I'm saying?

Don't try to base a relationship around fucking. Base your fucking around a relationship. Don't get it twisted, a good fuck has value, but it's nowhere near the basis for playing house. You may be trying to define something that needs no definition. Once you take this deal to the next level, you create rules and boundaries that neither of you may like nor respect. For the time being, I think you should leave things as they are, just let it flow. Enjoy it while it lasts!

"Hit it and quit it"   **--Folks**

Ask a player

Dear Player,

I am thinking about becoming a stripper. My sister is a dancer and she makes $400.00 - $500.00 a day, sometimes $900.00 - $1,200.00 on Fridays and Saturdays. I don't want to go to school for four years to end up making $700.00 a week. Should I do it? I value your opinion.

-J'Michia, 18, Newark, NJ

Dear Wantstitute,

I'm sure this sounds like a good deal, and you want yours now. However, nothing beats an education. In view of your age and lack of experience you may not want to make such a life altering decision just yet. Even if you become a stripper, you will need enough education to know how to take a stripping career to the next level. Everyone needs a plan B, NOT to be confused with Booty.

Trust me; I have nothing against a career in the adult entertainment industry. I'm just saying. Don't count anything out at this point. Make your own decision. Don't let money decide for you. Try going to school and stripping on the side to begin with. Being a stripper may not be all you think it is, check it out. Somehow you just don't sound like real ho material.

On the other hand, stripping may be your forte. There is a lot of money to be made in that industry, but it takes a special kind of woman to get it. "Everything is not for everybody." You may not want all of your eggs in one booty basket. Again, I say, check it out. Have a heart to heart with your sister. She knows things she has not told you. Trust me. Get the "Butt Naked Truth" first.

"You need to know 4 sho if you wanna ho. -**Folks**

Dear Readers,

I recently received a letter from a good friend I met in Federal Prison... My main man, Big Al Franklin. Big Al and I walked down a couple years together in Federal Prison at Edgefield, S.C. Big Al helped give birth to both my book and the idea for my film. Al's letter/poem touched me and I wanted to share it:

Dear Player,

I've come across a lot of fake shit in my life, some expensive, most cheap. I never knew a friendship could be so real until you introduced yourself to me. You're like an uncle, mentor and

guide. I was fortunate to meet the real Player inside. And now that I sit and reflect, not a moment do I regret listening and learning from one so wise. Under no circumstances would he compromise the game he learned, played and taught so well. It created the original from within a cell, one who proves to be more doer than sayer. I tip my hat to you, an all time Player.
--Big Al Washington, D.C's Finest

Prison friendships tend to be tighter and last longer than casual friendships. The reason for the quality of these types of friendships is based on the fact that in prison you see a person 7 days a week, 24 hours a day. Therefore, you get to know the real person... in the raw. If you can like someone under those types of adverse circumstances, seeing them with no pretenses, you are truly friends with that person.   -- Folks

Dear Player,

I have sex with more women than men. This is because my man and I have frequent threesomes. I always have the same man, but the women change all the time. I enjoy these women as much, if not more, than my man. Does this mean I'm gay?

-Jacquella, 27, Bonne Terre, Mo

The Original White Folks

Dear Big Fun with More than One,

Some form of this question surfaces at least once a month. As usual, my answer is that you are not gay if you like women yet have a man. Gay women don't do men, at all, under any circumstances. Therefore, you are bisexual because you have and enjoy sex with both men and women. Because you have the heart and realism to admit you thoroughly enjoy sex with both genders you are looked down upon by a bunch of frustrated, unrealistic prudes. Most women throw around the word *gay* in reference to sexually liberated women. You deserve applause for choosing to disregard the Suzie homemaker syndrome and enjoy sex to the fullest. You go girl!

Life is too short to go around with a stick up your ass and miss out on the incredible pleasures of sexual exploration. Women are sexual creatures by nature, and should feel free to enjoy their natural inclinations. Do not feel bad for doing what comes natural to you. Feel bad for those who live in fear of reality and are sexually frustrated. You lick'em like you like em girl! You're not gay. You're just a lot of fun! I'm sure your man is a happy camper and you seem to be one as well. Who gives a flying fuck on a rolling donut what the rest of em' think?

"Forgive them for they know not what they are missing"

--Folks

Dear Player,

I live a relatively conservative lifestyle. I have a college education, work in the corporate world and until recently, maintained a monogamous relationship with a boyfriend, with whom I lived. However, I have, what is considered by most as, wild fantasies/desires. I like to dress up like a stripper, put on shows and I want to get paid for my time and services. The idea of having sex for free doesn't sit well with me. On the other hand, I don't want to work in a strip club or be an outright prostitute either. Is there a middle ground where I can fit in and do my thing? Please help me solve my dilemma. It's very frustrating.

-Always been a hoe, 29, Denver, Co

The Original White Folks

Dear Wantstitute,

You are faced with a dilemma large numbers of women experience. The difference between you and most other women is that you feel a need to do something about it. It's commendable that you not only wish to act upon your instincts, but you are seeking the counsel of someone who actually knows the subject matter. Good move. You have the *only* "product" in the universe you can sell and still keep. PUSSY! You can sell it high. You can sell it low. You can even line up fifty guys and give it away. Pussy still retains its original value. Whole people come out of those things and they snap right back into shape! The maintenance on a vagina is extremely inexpensive as well. A gallon of vinegar, a case of Ivory soap and a few boxes of tampons will maintain a coochie for a year.

Now, couple that information with the fact that 98% of all men are total suckers when it comes to women and sex. Men's inability to control their sexual desires and their general weakness for women, are what make strip clubs one of the fastest growing businesses in America. Thus, if a woman has the heart, game and willingness to take advantage of all of the above factors she will do very well financially.

Ask a player

Now we come to the important part of the deal... The game required to accomplish this end. In your case, you are in need of the game to make your inner needs and desires happen in a discreet manner, in order to maintain your corporate image. How do we let the ho out without blowing your image? My first suggestion is for you to have a heart-to-heart talk with a real player and/or a real ho and explain the situation you are faced with, talk about what you want to do. I know that's what you are attempting to do with this question. However, you need a serious back and forth conversation in which you can get rapid answers to rapid questions. There is no quick "one liner" I can give for your situation.

I can make a couple of suggestions. Without knowing whether you are more interested in role playing, getting money from boyfriends or becoming a true undercover prostitute, I'm not sure where to take you. If your deal is the role-playing, you can usually explain that to almost any man. If you are trying to get money from boyfriends I suggest you start with a new boyfriend. My reason for saying that is that you usually end up the way you start off. So, if you're not getting paid now, the people you are dealing with are not going to be willing to start paying you at this late date. Clean house first. Then, you have to keep the first three rules of the game at the forefront of your mind:

The Original White Folks

1. Get the money up front. 2. Get the money up front and 3. Get the money up front!

When you deal with men, you have to make it known in no uncertain terms that they have only two ways to deal with you: Your way or the wrong way! Assert yourself. My last series of suggestions deals with you being that real ho you've been hiding. It's mentally un-healthy to have a part of your personality bottled up too long. You can work for an escort service. They pay well. You can create your own web site, wear a mask, block your face, or do live web-cam sex with males/females or both for big bucks. Become a dominatrix. That' extreme dress-up involving the use of leather face-masks, leather spiked bra and panties, whips, cat of nine tails, chains and hand cuffs. These are but a few of the wonderful toys of the trade. The mask is perfect for you, and it pays better than "normal" prostitution.

You need to make a big girl decision, whether you want a boyfriend, a trick or a player. You can't have them all in one or even two of them in one. A lame boyfriend can only teach you lame shit. If you walk with lames you will limp. A trick will pay you, but will not teach you to do better. A player will teach you how to deal with any situation and how to get paid in the process.

"Ho up or Blow up! -**Folks**

103

Ask a player

Dear Player,

When/how should I tell my new male friend/sex partner that I have a girlfriend too? My girlfriend and I have been together off and on for over 10 years. I recently met a man who really peaks my interest. I wonder what, if anything should be said at this stage of our relationship? He's not really my boyfriend yet, but... **—Sadie M., 34, Miami, Fl.**

Dear Lick em' & Stick em',

Well, it seems that you have considerable feelings for Mr. "not really my boyfriend." You obviously want to tell boyfriend about your affinity for fish, but you don't know how he will receive it. However, your attempt to "keep it real" is too little, too late. How about starting at the beginning? The better question would be when will you tell girlfriend about your diversion with dicks? You see, telling Mr. "not really my boyfriend" about your girlfriend will be of little benefit if girlfriend doesn't know about, or accept "not really my boyfriend" being in your life.

Ideally, both of your sex/love interests should be aware of each other. Both of them should care enough for your sexual needs and desires to make it a threesome. Of course, some women who desire other women sexually have no interest in men under any circumstances. On the other hand, it's near impossible to find a man who will pass up an opportunity to engage in a fuck fest with a couple of females. Therefore, I suggest you re-think your position and work on making this two-way/three-way "thing" of yours OK with your girlfriend first. If you having a boyfriend or even a male sex partner is unacceptable to your girlfriend, you may end up with neither fish nor beef. I'm sure, after ten years with girlfriend, you know her feelings on this subject. In fact, I wouldn't be surprised that your desire for dick is, at least, partially responsible for you and girlfriend's off and on relationship over the years. At any rate, you need to get your shit together. "Work on your mind first, your ass last"

--Folks

Dear Player,

I am a former intravenous heroin user. I've been clean for more than 5 years. My cousin is a crack head, but actually puts me down. She seems to think that being a current crack head is some how "better" than being a former dope-fiend. Her claim to fame is that she "doesn't shoot dope." My cousin has succeeded in making me feel bad. Should I?

Ask a player

-Tonya Wells, 39, Detroit

Dear Hung up Your Guns,

Hell No! It takes an ill mind to even think, much less actually believe, that a current drug abuser is somehow "better" than a former drug abuser, especially one who currently uses no drugs at all. That is asinine! I have lived in the streets over 40 years. Believe me. I have seen every form of substance abuser known to mankind. I have abused a few drugs myself. There **is** a difference between dope-fiends and crack heads.

Let's deal with the nuts and bolts of each addiction first. Crack is a derivative of cocaine. Cocaine is an "upper" causing the user to become hyper. The effects of cocaine are short-lived causing the user to need more coke immediately to maintain the desired effect. So, there is a constant state of desperation experienced by crack heads between rocks. On the other hand, heroin is a "downer." The user/abuser is slowed down and has more time to think. Heroin has long-term effects (high). Thus, a dope-fiend, heroin addict, has the luxury of sitting still long enough to come up with a few slick moves, whereas, crack heads are moving at 100 miles per hour in an 25 mile per hour zone. They do most things on impulse to get an immediate result.

Additionally, $50.00 will just get a crack head started. The same fifty will keep a heroin user high all day.

These facts are but a few of the reasons why a number of crack heads live under expressway overpasses, in shelters and "abandonminuims" (abandoned buildings). Crack heads panhandle, wash car windows at intersections and have sex outdoors for a couple bucks. Crack heads have also been known to have sex with multiple partners for a rock, which has been reported to include doing dogs and small farm animals.

Although some heroin users have been guilty of this sort of debauchery, it is done on a far less frequent basis than crack heads. Heroin users dress better, have slicker moves, own more property and possessions and, more importantly, have and act with far more morality and decorum than crack heads. I could go on and on with the differences, but I believe I've got my point across. In general, crack heads don't give a flying fuck on a rolling donut what they have to do to get a rock. The only thing they are afraid of is running out of rocks. Notwithstanding all of this information, your cousin is a crack head and thus, turns all of her money into a cloud of smoke. You are a former addict and use your money to better your life.

Let me simplify the argument, however stupid it may be, it doesn't make one bit of difference what part of your body you put your drugs in, or no matter what brand of drugs you use; Whether you drink it, shoot it, snort it, smoke it or put it in a chair and suck it up through your asshole. If you are addicted to drugs you're a dope-fiend, point blank! There is no glory in any drug use/abuse. All drugs destroy both brain cells and internal organs. Some drugs cause more damage than others, but it's all stupid and suicidal. Why do you think they call it dope? Just say NO! I have to question your thought pattern for allowing this stupid shit to become an issue for you. Get on with your life and leave the petty stuff to petty people. There is an old saying that comes to mind here:

"When a fool and a wise person argue, it's hard to tell which is which."

--Folks

Dear Player,

My boss is a flaming asshole. As a Player, how would you deal with ignorant people in a corporate environment?

-Want to beat up my boss, Lexington, KY.

The Original White Folks

Dear Corporate Thug,

Don't do it! As a player I would not "deal" with an ignorant person period. However, if I found a need to "deal" with a damned fool, I would play past them. I believe your problem here is that you are trying to achieve some form of harmony with an idiot. You should treat your boss as a computer, i.e. feed him the necessary information to perform a function. Do not expect anything back other than raw information to perform your function. Do or say only what is absolutely necessary. Do not express any opinions either positive or negative. For god's sake, don't do anything in violation of the rules. No tardiness or unexplained absences. In other words, you should go along to get along.

Last, but certainly not least, if I were you, I would find myself another job, one in which I could feel comfortable and at ease. Peace of mind and comfort cannot be replaced by prestige or position. Being happy with whatever you do is the key to a long, prosperous life and good mental health. These are but a few of the reasons that prompted me to become a player. I'm allergic to bullshit!

"If it don't fit find one that does"   **--Folks**

Ask a player

Dear Player,

My live-in boyfriend and I recently broke up, but he doesn't seem to want to leave. I told him I want him to move, but he's not hearing it. We are still having sex. That does not mean I want him back or that we can continue living together. I don't want to call the police to get him out. I'm pretty sure he has warrants. *What can I do to get him to take me seriously?*
-Niah, 26, Houston

Dear You Can't be Serious,

I'm happy to hear that at least one black woman has the wherewithal to keep the police out of their personal business. You didn't call anyone to get this relationship started and you're not going call for help to end it. BIG "ups" to you sister. However, just when you made a responsible decision, you committed an astronomical error. I don't really want to call you stupid after making such a big girl decision regarding the police, but how can you actually expect a man, with whom you live, to take you seriously about moving when you give him a blowjob in one breath and try to blow him off in the next? Stop Playin!

"Drop the dick and step away from it"   **--Folks**

Dear Player,

My boyfriend asked me if he could stay with me until he gets on his feet. We have been together for about three months, but I've known him for a couple of years. He hasn't had a job, visible means of support or any money since I've known him. I really think I can help him though. Do you think this is a good idea?

- Treana, 24, Washington D.C.

Dear Tre-Wanna-Man Without a Plan,

First of all, I feel it necessary to take notice of the fact that this man hasn't had any money, doesn't have any, nor does he seem to possess a plan to have any in the foreseeable future. This set of circumstances is obviously not a problem for you. Therefore, it is equally obvious that you simply want a man for the sake of saying you have one... sort of like a human dildo.

Secondly, it appears you have taken this "opportunity" to have your dick and eat it too. Your boyfriend has no job, money or hustle. Thus, you can only be interested in sex. Hell, there is not much else to be desired here. Well Miss Hot Stuff, you will not get me to help you justify this lame ass move you are trying to make. If you are that dick hungry you will come out a lot better calling a male escort. Give him $150.00-$200.00 and have yourself a ball, (no pun intended.) Such a move will be a lot cheaper than trying to feed, sleep and clothe a grown man; Maybe even buy him a car or end up standing outside your job waiting on him to show up with yours.

However, if being able to throw a party for your pussy on demand is your idea of relationship bliss, look no further. On the other hand, if you are looking to grow, as a woman, prosper as a person, have children with a real father, or own anything real, you are fucking up big time! Pay more attention to your life than your ass. No one else will.

"Bullshit is only good for growing a garden"

--**Folks**

Dear Player,

My sister ain't spoke to me in 5 years; since I told her I thought she was a fool to marry her then boyfriend, now her husband. Now I feel like the fool. My sister is happily married to the same guy. I miss my sister. I've tried to apologize but she keeps hanging up on me. How can I get her to listen?

-**Sharon P., 28, Cleveland, Tenn.**

Dear Need to Mind Your Own Business,

Send her a copy of this column. Without more information about your sister and her character, I cannot supply you with an adequate answer.

"If you properly handle all of your business, there will be no time left in the day to dip into anyone else's." **--Folks**

Dear Player,

I have a 3-year-old little girl. I recently broke up with my live-in boyfriend, not my baby's daddy. So, I don't have a man in my life right now. I have this male friend who is having a really hard time. He is fine as hell, has a promising music career, but has nowhere to stay until he gets his first check in two weeks. We don't have a relationship and we haven't had sex. We're just friends. Should I let him sleep on my couch until he gets his first check? I just want to help him.

-Kristen, 26, Houston

Dear Mama from the Lost Man Mission,

A significant part of the answer to your question can be found in this column. See the answer to Tre-Wanna-Man's question. However, your question does require additional comment. Your live-in boyfriend, who is not your child's father, has come and gone. I'm sure your daughter feels that void in her life, as well as yourself. You need to look at the message you will be sending your female child with all of the men coming and going. There seems to be a lot of activity with you and men. Let's get real here. You don't have a man, think this guy is "fine as hell" and you're apparently used to having a man around. You are trying to use this fake ass "help him" shit to "help yourself." Even if Mr. Fine gets a check in two weeks, will that check pay for a security deposit, rent, furniture, dishes, food, pots, pans and transportation?

I believe you are blinded by the need/desire for a man. You honestly don't see where this "two week" stay is going? Or is it that you just don't care as long as there is a dick attached to the deal? Come on now girlfriend. Step back and take a long hard look at yourself, your life and the future of your child. You are responsible for shaping the life, future and thought pattern of another human being, act accordingly!

"Buy yourself real sex toys   **--Folks**

Dear Player,

I am sick and tired of you glorifying and praising this so-called game of yours. You are rude, obnoxious and have filthy language.

-Lulu Mae Williams, 48, St. Louis

Dear Hater,

You obviously suffer from some rare mental defect. IF YOU DON'T LIKE IT, SIMPLY DON'T READ THE COLUMN. YOU ARE INCREDIBLY STUPID!! You have clearly not read my disclaimer at the beginning of this column. Check under my photo. Your reading skills are as bad as your thinking ability. I have a 1st Amendment right to freedom of speech. I can say whatever I want. You have a similar right not to read it. Exercise your rights and leave mine alone.

"I think you secretly like me."   **--Folks**

Dear Player,

I have had several men complain that my coochie is too big. I usually respond by telling them that maybe the problem is that their dick is too little. But really, I've heard this complaint so

many times I am taking it serious. Is there anything I can do to tighten up by business?
-Anonymous-
Dear Too Big for Your Britches,

There is an old trick used by prostitutes to solve your particular problem. I first heard about it in the sixties and it was an old trick then. The solution involves the use of a powder called *Alum,* [Aluminum oxide]which was available at pharmacies. The Alum powder is used in a warm water douche and insto-presto you're almost a virgin again! I am unaware of whether Alum is still sold. However, a conversation with your local pharmacist will answer that question. In view of Alum being an old remedy, it may have been replaced with something new and improved. Again, check with your local drug store. A conversation with an old ho may net you some very valuable information as well.

There are also a number of vaginal exercises which are helpful in the tightening process. The *Kegel* exercises are good for strengthening vaginal muscles. It's the repetitive clenching and releasing of the vaginal muscles. The practice of stopping your urine mid-stream is very helpful. Pregnant women are instructed in this practice. Last, but by no means least, we have the ancient Ben-Wah balls.

These balls can be purchased at adult novelty stores. The Ben-Wah balls have been used in the Orient since the beginning of time. They consist of two small balls that are inserted vaginally. The objective is to make them rotate around internally through the clenching and release of the vaginal muscles. Once the ability to make them rotate has been achieved, then maximum coochie control has been mastered.

Hopefully this information will enable you to get that thing tight as fish pussy, and that's waterproof!

--Folks

Dear Player,

    I've been doing research on the game. I have read Iceberg Slim, Donald Goines, Bilbo and a few others, including your book. Most notably I recently read two books; one entitled *Pimpin Ain't Easy* by Keith Curtis and another titled *The Mack Within* by King Flex. Both of these authors used the term "Captain save-a-ho." In addition, both of these authors attribute this terminology to a rapper named E-40, who used the phrase in a 1990s rap song. I read that same phrase in your book. My point is that most of your writing is old school. I don't think you are quoting rappers, but correct me if I'm wrong. In fact, most rappers seem to be quoting guys like

you in their songs. My question is, from whom, where or when did the phrase *Captain save-a-ho* come from?

-Marcus Williams, Bookstore owner, Southlake Mall, Morrow, GA   (NUBIAN BOOKSTORE)

Game, Bullshit or Blasphemy?

You came to the right place for an answer. Among a host of other titles I hold, I am a game historian. In fact, I also hold a Ph D (Pimp-ho Degree) in street life. Like most situations or questions regarding life or the game, if you want a genuine, bona fide answer, **ASK A PLAYER!** In direct answer to your question, the term *Captain save-a-ho* has been used by pimps and players since the 1940s. My uncle Rocky, 77 years old, who was pimping in the late 40s, and from whom I got the game in the 1960s, used that terminology at least 30 years before E-40 or these guys were born. This kind of confusion, misconception and misinformation being disseminated by people commercializing the game is one of my pet peeves. My books and, more so, my film, Original Game Reloaded! deal directly with this sort of bastardizing and de-valuing of the game, what it stands for and represents. The last two or three generations of young people are getting what they think is game off the stage, from people who are not pimps or players, but claim or pretend to be. Most of these rappers, that claim to be pimps in their songs, couldn't be a pimple on a pimp's ass! These rappers and/or their songwriters pick up sayings, statements, or slogans from real pimps and players in the streets, and claim them as their own.

A great number of people in the rap game have made a multi-million dollar industry out of claiming or pretending to be pimps and players. Meanwhile, those of us who are the genuine article, pimped and played for an entire lifetime, go without proper recognition as pimps and players. The really sad part of this incredibly fake shit is that it's selling, and young people are patterning their lives around this bullshit. The situation has gotten so critical that people are now writing books and making films about pimps and players, claiming to be experts and quoting rappers as a reference point for game. [Note: E-40 never claimed ownership]

The rappers have stolen, excuse me..."sampled", these very same quotes from genuine pimps and players. What happened to the *real*? Thus, you have one group of people who actually believe they are players based upon bullshit, slogans, rhymes and rap songs. These people are disseminating books, making films and claiming to be experts on a subject that they obtained from the entertainment industry. Then you have another group of people, who believe this rhetoric, buy it and try to live it. There you have the demise and death of true game. The blind are leading the blind! What happened to genuine game? Where's the real?

For the record, real game is passed down from one generation of players to the next. The aforementioned is a perfect example of why I constantly insist that if you didn't get your game from an old school player you don't have game... you have bullshit! Most people don't seek the truth because they simply can't handle the truth! The rest of them don't know the truth exists. I guess that's why bullshit is selling at an astronomical rate, and the *real* lies dormant on the shelves. Who knew?

I've done a little research of my own on the books/authors you made reference to. Just as a measure of proof of my statements here, I would like to point out that Keith Curtis also authored a book entitled "*The American Males Guide on How to Get More Pussy.*" It's nearly impossible for me to see how one can be an expert on both pimping and tricking at the same time! Pimping is a paper chase. **The *pursuit of pussy* is a trick activity.** I don't know where he is going with this. Is he an expert on pimping or tricking? He needs to pick one subject on which he's an expert. At least one of these books, by its sheer nature, has to be pure, unadulterated bullshit! However, both of his books seem to do well. This is the result of the lack of true game and the demise of the original rules of the game. When your main focus is pussy, all you can expect is to **get fucked!** Even though professional Pimp words like Game, Ism and out of pocket are thrown around... At least King Flex doesn't disrespect the game to the point of calling himself a pimp. Credit due for Hidden Colors... he made a career out of what he does, and gets money. +

"When you bite Game... It bites back!" Grr   **-Folks**

Dear Player,

   I started college in Atlanta this year. The first thing I noticed was that credit card companies sent me several pre-approved credit card applications. All of my friends and other students, I know, got these pre-approved credit card applications. I didn't sign or mail any of the credit card applications back. If I did, how would I pay for them? I'm a full time student with no job. Is this game? I'm sure that it is. Please explain what the business is?
   -Sharlisa G., 19, Tampa, Fl

Ask a player

Dear Know it when You See It,

You hit the nail dead on the head! The practice you described is a part of some of the biggest game played in this country! College students possess the raw materials to make changes in the system. Students have the potential to be a monkey wrench in the machinery, so to speak. So, long-range game is played to weed out at least a good number of poor and disenfranchised students. Here is how the game works. Only the poor and underprivileged students are in need of credit cards. The people with money already have them. First, from a purely business standpoint, why would a credit card company give a full time student, with no job, a credit card? How is that student supposed to pay for it?

When you get this pre-approved card and begin to enjoy the opportunity to purchase items you normally could not afford, you have to get a part-time job to pay the bill. Once you have paid the bill, several more credit card companies will send you more pre-approved credit card offers. Now, you have to work more hours on your part-time job to stay current on your new credit card payments. After paying several of the new bills you get pre-approved auto loan applications in recognition of your newfound credit status… Gotta get that whip!

Once you have accepted this new car loan, you will need more hours at work in order to pay your car note. Of course, at this juncture, your grades begin to fall because you have very little time or energy to study. At this point, you have to reassess your position regarding whether you want or need to stay in school. You have credit cards, a new car and a job. Hell, you're doing better than your parents, or so you think. They don't even have a new car. This is where, at least, some students decide to drop out of school and join the work force full time. These students do not want to give up their newfound credit status or the new car. Not to speak of the fact that their grades have fallen to an unacceptable level anyway. If you don't pay the credit card bill you are out of the running for having credit for at least seven years, you can't buy a home, more cars, get an apartment or open a bank account.

Now you are doomed to be an underpaid, overtaxed employee for the rest of your life. Employers don't have to pay you much because you don't have much education. Big business and the Government are the beneficiaries of this move. Big business has gained a lifetime employee, and the government has gained a low income, highly taxable citizen. The proof that big business and big government are co-conspirators in this move, big business will take part of your money and hold it for their partner, the Government. Hopefully, I have adequately answered your question.   **--Folks**

Dear Player,

   I had a car accident, and my vehicle was totaled. The other driver involved in the accident was at fault and received a traffic ticket for crossing over into my lane. My insurance company wants to pay for my vehicle, but they will take out a $500.00 deductible. I don't think it's fair for me to have to pay a $500.00 deductible for an accident that was not my fault. Shouldn't the other driver's insurance pay in full?

-Rocky Reed, 78, Atlanta

Dear Banged Up and Screwed Over,

   You are absolutely correct. You should not, nor do you have to pay a deductible under the circumstances of your auto accident. The insurance carrier of the culprit in your mishap is totally responsible for any damages to your person and/or vehicle. This responsibility includes your deductible as well. The whole idea and law behind the responsibility of the insurance carrier of the driver at fault, is that the innocent victim should not have to pay for being victimized. Thus, the other person's insurance provider has to pay your deductible and any other costs or injury you may have incurred, as a result of the accident.

Therefore, you need to obtain a copy of the police report, which will contain the other driver's name, insurance provider's name and his/her insurance policy number. Armed with this information, you should contact the other driver's insurance company and file a claim with them for the full amount of your loss and/or injury including your deductible. They are legally responsible to pay all costs.

"When you can't quite figure it out, seek the real...

"Ask a player!" **--Folks**

Dear Player,

I am almost 50 years old and I am thinking about going back to school. I never got my high school diploma. I want to do something about it, but I'm a little embarrassed. I feel stupid and I will probably be the only grandmother in class seeking a GED.

-Shirley Banks, 48, Little Falls, Minn.

Ask a player

Dear Graduating Granny,

Big Ups to you girlfriend! It's never too late. There is an old saying in the game: *"Game don't stop till the casket drop."* The same applies to the need for education. The pursuit of knowledge is power. Don't ever forget that! From a realistic standpoint, I believe it is much more embarrassing to be under-educated than it is to be seeking enlightenment at any age. Knowledge is power. Everyone should seek as much knowledge/power as they possibly can. Do not feel bad because you got a late start. Save the pity for those who lack the common sense that they need to continue their education. You are on the right path. Don't let anyone, bitch, bulldog or baby, including yourself, prevent you from growing as a person. You go Girl!

"May the force be with you"   **--Folks**

Dear Player,

I am a professional prostitute and madame. I own an internet escort service. I have a question of which I cannot seem to get an adequate answer. Why is it that the same women

who's claim to fame is *"I ain't no hoe, I don't sell pussy,"* are perfectly content to give away pussy to every Tom, Dick and Harry? The really stupid part of these free fucking tramp's thoughts, is that they believe they are somehow better than real hoes that get paid. You would think that a woman such as myself would know the answer to this question, but I don't. Do you?

-Honey Falls, Chicago's finest

Dear Have No Praise for Passing Pussy,

As much as I hate to admit it, I don't know the answer either. However, I have a damn good, educated, working hypothesis. The "give away" crew is lost in the Rebecca of Sunnybrook Farm, middle class, white American myths of morality, fair play and the spoon fed "American Dream" bullshit society forces upon us. We are taught this false sense of moral right and wrong from childhood. Society does this to stifle independent thought. We are taught to "do the right thing" and follow the rules. Of course, this train of thought leaves no room for advancement, self preservation, entrepreneurship or just plain doing what you have to do in order to get where you want to be. Under those circumstances, the brainwashed bitches following society's so called rules and morality end up playing themselves. These women honestly believe that being a free fucking tramp is better than being a paid ho because it's "socially acceptable." Kind of like Santa Claus, the Easter Bunny, the Tooth Fairy and Knights in Shining Armor.

What these lame ass women fail to realize is that being broke is even more socially unacceptable than being anything or anyone else. A ho with money will have her ass kissed like royalty in places like Trump Plaza, Caesars Palace and Bellagio in Vegas, or any other five-star establishment. Guess what five-star establishments will do for a morally fit, socially acceptable broke ass bitch whose claim to fame is "I don't sell pussy?" You got it! She will be tossed out on her free fucking ass!

When you buy a home, car, mink coat or when paying your electric, gas, cable or internet bills, you are never asked where or how you got the money. However, if you don't have it, you will be disconnected! To be or not to be becomes the question of the day. Ho up or blow up! Don't get it twisted here. I'm not saying that all women should sell pussy. I am pointing out that selling pussy beats the hell out of being homeless, in the dark, having no heat, phone, cable, transportation etc. etc. See what I'm saying? There is no glory in being broke. Right is no better than wrong if it doesn't work.

The Original White Folks

"Think outside the box... it will keep you in the house"   **-- Folks**

Dear Player,

I want to make a sex film of me and my boyfriend because the thought of it excites me. My concern is that someone else might see the tape. I am confused, but I really want to do it. What do you think I should do?

-J'Isha, 23, Springfield, Ill

Dear Porn Star Wannabe,

Don't do it! If you have a serious fear of anyone seeing your fuck fest on film debut, the **ONLY** way to guarantee no one sees it is if it doesn't exist. Otherwise, there is always a possibility of the film being viewed by someone other than you. Think about how many celebrities' embarrassing film footage you've seen on T.V or the Internet. See what I mean?

"No one can see what's not there."   **-- Folks**

Dear Player,

I saw a T.V. program on 60 Minutes about the "Stop Snitchin" Movement. I'm sorry, but I don't think I could live next door to a serial killer or child molester and not tell the police. Am I wrong for that?
-Patricia Patton, 31, Las Vegas

Dear Run and Tell It,

I understand your desire to have serial killers, child molesters and the like removed from your community. Hell, I don't want those types of deranged people in my neighborhood either. However, the Stop Snitchin Movement is not intended for the protection of persons who indiscriminately, kill, molest children or commit other heinous or senseless crimes. Snitching, as applied to street life or the game, targets people who testify on their friends, relatives and competitors as a means of lessening a criminal sentence or for financial gain.

The intended target of the Stop Snitchin Movement speaks to persons who voluntarily engage in criminal activity with full knowledge of the consequences. It refers the so-called player who, upon being arrested and expected to accept

130

punishment for his actions, tells on his friends and relatives, or a "player" who snitches on his competition in order to corner the market in his hood.

Last, but certainly not least, we have the snitch that simply does it for pay. These types of snitches are a long way from being good Samaritans or citizens in fear of their lives or those of their children.

There is a gigantic difference between being a witness and snitching. Witnesses are citizens that see, hear, or have knowledge of a crime and report it. A snitch is a participant in a crime, who labels himself a player, yet betrays his friends, violates the code by which he lives, gives up his manhood and all he claims to stand for and represent in the process. Basically they become a BITCH! We pay law enforcement on the federal, state and local levels to catch the bad guys. However, they tell us it is our "civic duty" to help them do it. A Perfect example: America's most wanted, etc. That's a pretty good deal. I wish I could get paid for a job and have someone else do the work. It sounds better than pimping to me. Run and tell that!

The bottom line here is that I'm trying to provide you another outlook on the Stop Snitchin Movement. The whole point is if anyone volunteers to be a criminal i.e. Thug, player etc. and gets busted, these persons should take their own weight!

Stop portraying the part of a thug or player, and then become a BITCH when it's no longer convenient to claim being a player. Pick one or the other suckas!

"STOP SNITCHIN!"   **--Folks**

Dear Player,

What is the "gap" between a woman's legs that I hear so many men make reference to?
-J'Nashia, 24, Northside- Chicago

Dear Wanna Rap about the Gap,

The "gap" you are inquiring about is the space between usually tall and/or thin women's legs. This space is otherwise closed at the point where women's thighs come together and touch. However, the owner of a "gap" has thighs which never come together or touch at the pelvic area. Therefore, when a woman with a "gap" stands with legs together, light can be seen coming through, at the coochie area from both the front or rear view... like a lighthouse beacon. This is a very sexually suggestive appearance to men. Of course, such a look has no bearing on sexual activity or the frequency thereof. It's simply sexy to most men.

"Follow the light at the end of the tunnel"   **--Folks**

Dear Player,

I was riding with my dad one day when we saw an obviously gay woman (baggy men's clothing, low hair cut, swaggering walk) holding hands with a very feminine looking woman. The woman in men's clothing was conspicuously pregnant. My dad went ballistic! He said that the obviously gay woman's pregnancy is a slap in the face of both men and lesbians alike. What's up with his outrage? I hope you know because I can't figure it out.

–Malikah J, 21 Detroit

Dear Want to Know Why Dad Don't Like the Dyke,

In general, men are insulted by women posing as, acting like or giving the appearance of being a man. This feeling of insult is based upon the fact that manhood is a state of being achieved through hard work, knowledge and life experience which can only be accomplished by a male. Therefore, when a man witnesses a woman trying to imitate him, it's a slap in the face of manhood. The average man thinks to himself: How in hell can a woman think so little of manhood or believe it to be so shallow that she thinks she is able to duplicate or imitate man with a look, an attitude and a dildo?

Your dad's ballistic outrage can be explained by the above train of thought, coupled with the pregnancy of the lesbian woman you and your dad saw. That pregnancy, in the opinion of the average man, is salt in the wound of insult, i.e. a lesbian woman, pretending to be a man, yet engaging in the ultimate act of womanhood... childbearing. A pregnant dyke...? This expands the phrases, brazen audacity, unmitigated gall, oxymoron, confusion and stupidity to the 10th power! The average male never reaches real manhood. Understand what I'm saying? Can you spell sheep in wolf's clothing? That's my opinion and I'm sticking to it.

"It's not nice to fool Mother Nature." **--Folks**

The Original White Folks

Dear Player,

Is there any truth to the rumor that you are the character named White Folks in Iceberg Slim's book *Trick Baby*?

-Iisac Waller, 48, Indianapolis

Dear Wanna Get it Right,

I get this question a lot. Hopefully, I will dispel the myth & mystery by answering your question in this column. No, I am not the character in Iceberg's book. That White Folks was fictional. I explained this mystery in my book *Original Game*. In fact, I will quote from my book in answer to your question and the unasked, "Super Fly" question. "I have been called "White Folks" since 1959. Thus, I had the moniker at least ten years before Iceberg Slim's *Trick Baby* book, whose main character was a half white/black con man named "White Folks." I have not attempted to look or act like "Super Fly", who was played by Ron O'Neal in a 1971-72 movie. Ron O'Neal was acting out a part in a movie, reading a script. The part, played by Ron, was based on a composite of pimps, dope dealers, and hustlers, like myself and others in the game. Therefore, Ron O'Neal was made up to look and act like me and my kind. Ron was an actor. THIS is the life I live every day. Who's imitating whom?"

To expand this answer, I will point out the fact that Iceberg Slim's character was an adult in the 1940's, which was before I was born. In addition, Iceberg's character was blonde with blue eyes. I have brown eyes and hair. There are a number of players and pimps in the game who use some variation of the name, "White Folks." Some of these guys are white, and some are half white, such as myself. Therefore, in an effort to distinguish myself from the growing numbers of others, I am called "Original White Folks." In view of the fact that I have had the name since 1959, I believe I qualify for "*The Original* "as a prefix to my name. Most of the other "White Folks" were not even born when I acquired the name in early childhood. Therefore, they certainly didn't have the name over 50 years ago.

I recently applied for a Federal Trademark for the name "White Folks." Thus, no one can use the name commercially without my permission. So, not only am I the "Original White Folks," but I hold a Federal trademark in addition to my pre-existing Federal Copyright on the name. As far as the other people in the game with the same name, I have no ill feelings for them. It's no different than being

named John and having a problem with others named John. See what I mean? I simply Trademarked the name because I use my name commercially, and I have to distinguish myself from the ever growing number of other White Folks.
"It's not in the name, it's in the game."
I'm old... But not **that** old!   **--Folks**

Dear Player,

I am a light skinned sista, with no butt. I have been told that I am really pretty. I have DD boobs and a very small waist. I want a big butt to complete my "total package." I've heard rumors that having anal sex causes your butt to grow. Is there any truth to the rumor? I am willing to try, but I don't want to lose my virginity in that area based upon an unfounded rumor.

-Tynesha, 23, Milwaukee

Dear Don't Want to be Poked if it's a Joke,

I have heard these rumors most of my life and witnessed results on a number of women that employed this practice as a form of booty enhancement. There is no confirmed medical proof that butt fucking grows ass. However, there are a number of former victims of the "noassatall" disease who swear by this method. Notwithstanding the rumor, the act of anal sex requires the use of all your anus and butt muscles. Thus, anal sex necessarily includes an extreme rear end exercise regime that will strengthen and add bulk to those areas. So, at least in theory, having your *i* dotted does have the potential to grow muscle mass. There may be other forces at work in this activity as well. Maybe the injection of protein contributes to the process. Who really knows? Most rumors have some basis in fact. So, after all is said and done on this subject, I would suggest you give it a try. Get on your knees and do it "doggy style." Have your partner reach around and manipulate your clit while hitting the wrinkled bull's eye. You may as well have fun, even if you don't become Buffy the Body. You are guaranteed a payday one way or the other. If you're lucky, you may win in both races and both places. Get your weight up!

"The more you get hit the bigger it gets?" **--Folks**

Dear Player,

I am a young brother who wants to pimp 'til I die. I need to know what I am supposed to do when I don't have a ho?

-Denver Dave, 22, Denver, Co

Dear PI Till you DI... Need a Day Job,

First of all, let me point out that this is a newspaper column not a "how to" guide, notwithstanding the fact that pimping, despite what you may think, is illegal. It is not my purpose or intent, to condone, promote, encourage, justify or glorify criminal activity. I simply speak on the realness of game and street life. I do not, nor do I desire to, teach classes on the subject. That being said, pimping is **in** you, not **on** you! It has to be more than a fleeting thought or a cute idea in your fantasies. The fact that you don't know or have a clue as to the first step, (getting a ho) I suggest you keep your day job. Stay in your own lane.

"If you don't have a job, get one!"   **--Folks**

Dear Player,

All of you old school dudes talk about how bad the game has gotten and blame it on young players, hip hop, rappers and young people. When, and exactly and how, did the game go bad? Who is really at fault here? Think maybe you guys dropped the ball?

"That Guy" (Guy Barnes), 27, Pomona, Ca

Ask a player

Dear Wanna Know the Deal on the Real,

Your question is a very difficult one to answer. There are so many factors involved in the demise of the original game that it's hard to narrow them down to a newspaper column answer. As usual, I will give it my best shot. I will start with the segment of your question asking if we, old school players, dropped the ball. I can only speak from personal experience. However, I can say that there are a number of old school players, who could have made a difference but didn't. The top 5 reasons these players "dropped the ball" instead of passing it are:

1. Long prison sentences
2. Drug and alcohol abuse
3. Old age and illness
4. Unwillingness/selfishness
5. Fear of prosecution or persecution.

These are but a few of the reasons a lot of old school players did not pass the game along to the next generation. So, yes, to some degree old school players are due some of the blame for the sad state of today's Game. Nevertheless, even if the ball was fumbled, each new generation had an increasing unwillingness to listen to those of us who tried to pass on true polished game.

Young people considered what we were trying to tell them as out dated "old ass shit." Each new generation had, what they felt was, a new and improved, "better" idea. These "new Playas" were looking for improvements and short cuts in the game. The incredible error of this thought is that you can't improve or create a short cut to anything, unless you have full and complete knowledge of what that thing is. Ya'll wouldn't listen so we quit talking. We shouldn't have to go out, find and force-feed you the real. You should be looking for us, seeking out game. There is no fast-food method of learning or playing game.

Now that I have gotten that off my chest, I can answer the rest of your question. There are four major contributors to the beginning of the end of true polished game:

1. Drugs
2. Rap music's fake pimps & players
3. Cable TV
4. Snitching

I'm sure, as always, I will get a lot of criticism for this answer. (See my disclaimer).

Hopefully you can handle the truth. In the late 1960s and early 1970s, after black people rioted, looted and nearly burned several major cities to the ground, 1965 Watts, 1966 Newark, 1967 Detroit, 1968 Chicago, (Democratic National Convention), and expressed an unwillingness to "go along" with the program, heroin was mass dumped into the ghetto. A lot of the now old school players got hooked back then. In that era you could buy $1.00 capsules of heroin. Dope was cheaper than a bottle of wine. Then came crack in the early to mid 80's. This is where teenaged kids found that they could make large amounts of money without having any real game. This is also where young, so-called, "Playas" felt there was no need to seek the advice of old school players. They were "gettin money!"

Then came the Hip Hop movement, which was cool until rappers started lying, claiming and pretending to be pimps, players and gangsters. The real harm these fakes caused is the number of young people that believed the hype and tried to pattern their lives after the fake shit coming off the stage. They failed to realize that rapping is entertainment having little to no basis in fact or real life. Since no one tried to seek real game in the last few generations, no one knew the difference. Rappers made a multi-million dollar industry out of pretending or claiming to be pimps and players.

After two or three generations of fake pimps and players on TV, the genuine article, **real** pimps and players, have been lost in the sauce. The commercial brand is the order of the day. It's not real and no one seems to notice the difference. Keep it real? Yeah right. If this bullshit is your idea of what's real we are all doomed! Got game? Get it!

Cable TV made the bullshit brand of pimps and players available both far and wide, to every nook and cranny in every state in the union. Finally, we come to the snitching. Becoming a RAT is now at epidemic proportion. The reason for the current trend of mass snitching is due, in large part, to young Players that did not obtain their game from old school players. These snitches are the product of the "get your game off the stage" generation. We didn't teach that bullshit! Snitching is not game, its bitch shit! If you do it you are less than a man and much, much less than a player. That's why they are called **RATS.**

At the risk of being repetitious I have to reiterate my often written/spoken favorite fact: "If you didn't get your game from an old school player, you don't have game... you have bullshit!" Get your game up players!

Game is passed down from one generation of players to the next. You can't teach yourself something you have no knowledge of or history on. If you don't know where the game has been, how can you even dream you know where it's going or how to get there? This answer is but a drop in the bucket of where and how the game went sour. Keep game alive! Get copies of my other books.

"Got game? Get it!"   **--Folks**

Dear Player,

What does the term "gapper" mean? My father who thinks he is an old school player uses this term a lot. He even talks about one of his old friends named "Gapper Slim." I know its old school, street slang, but exactly what is the definition?

-Lloyd Parks Jr., 28, Los Angeles

Dear Rapper That Wants to Know About the Gapper,

The term *gapper*, as used by old school players, is derived from the word gap. Webster's dictionary defines gap as "an opening." The street adaptation of the word gap into the term gapper, describes the act of filling the gap, or opening in another person's pocket. This filling of the gap is an act best described as somewhat similar to a gratuity or tip for services rendered. For example, someone gives a player information, which proves useful in obtaining some fast, or a large sum of money, they are due a gapper. It's a token of appreciation.

There is another use in the streets for the term gapper. A gapper is also a gift of money given to a known player, who is doing bad, between moves or just plain down on his luck. It's kind of like the taxes a player pays to the less fortunate in the game. When a player is released from prison or jail he is due a gapper from other players. A pimp, whose last ho has run off, is due a gapper as well. Players use the gapper system to keep fellow players propped up until they can come up. The giving of a gapper is an important and necessary part of the game. It's the equivalent of unemployment benefits for players. If players don't support or aid each other who will? You see what I'm saying? The gapper deal is sort of like social services for players. The word may have changed over the years, but the practice still remains. Hopefully I have answered your question. Look out for your own. Thank you for your support.

"If you're in the game support the game"   **--Folks**

Dear Player,

I get a sexual charge from food, sex and money. Does that make me weird?

-Dortheah, 26, Seattle, Wa

Dear Sex, Money and Food freak,

If you add drugs and/or alcohol to the mix, you would be a perfectly normal Hollywood movie/ rock star. Who am I to rain on your parade?

"Go for it!"   **--Folks**

Dear Player,

Why is it that people who embrace the terms "Pimp & Player" seem to have so much real resentment toward the genuine article? The people I'm referring to all refer to themselves and their friends as pimps and players, but when they encounter a real pimp or player, they always have something negative to say. What is that all about?

-Darnell Johnson, 30, Dallas, Tx

Dear Wanna know about Suckers, Busters, Imitators and Haters,

146

The behavior you describe is standard procedure for the average lame. It's in their genes. They cannot help themselves. These are the people being referred to when you hear the term "Player Hater."

"If they knew better they would do better, but they don't, so they won't."

--Folks

Dear Player,

I've got a squad of freaks who hang around me on a regular. I do a few things, and I live large. The freaks do what I tell them. I have had my freaks hook my boyz up with sex all the time. I realize that my boyz will spend money on these hoes so I want to get paid for my girls. Tell me what I need to do with these whores so I can get my pimp on? These freaks do whatever I tell them for fun. Money should get them jumping 4 real. Hook a brotha up!
-Big Bee a/k/a Big Baller, St. Paul, Minn.

Dear Wanna Add Game to Shame,

First off, pimping as well as prostitution are both illegal, with the exception of brothels in the Nevada dessert outside of Las Vegas and Reno. It is obvious that your understanding of game, as well as law, is almost zero and leaves much to be desired. You are asking me, in a newspaper, to provide you with information and encouragement, with which you intend to use to commit the felony crime of pimping and pandering.

I might add that you are requesting of me, a total stranger, to become your co-defendant in a 20-year maximum felony crime, in a public newspaper no less. It seems here lately that I'm getting more requests for this sort of illegal advice. Let me make clear that I do not provide "how to" criminal advice. I offer player influenced, realistic advise to the general public regarding resolution of everyday issues and problems.

"Rethink what you are doing and more importantly how you are conducting your business."   **--Folks**

Dear Player,

I'm confused. I can't figure out why my boyfriend and his friends all call themselves "pimp" and "player". They all work every day and have families. None of these men have other women, and they know they had better not. In fact, most of them can't even handle the relationship they have. Please help me understand.
-Lucresha Coleman, 32, Kansas City, Kansas

The Original White Folks

Dear "Player's" Playmate,

Pimps and players are the most often imitated, but never duplicated, people on the planet. The most common reason for the average man's fascination with pimps and players are these person's lavish lifestyles and many pretty women. I wouldn't worry if I were you. As long as boyfriend is going to work and taking care of you let him have his fantasy. Everyone is entitled to dream. It's kind of like little boys that say they want to be "Superman" when they grow up.

"Some things are better left alone."   **--Folks**

Dear Player,

I enjoy shooting firearms and find it very relaxing. In fact, I would even say I find it to be therapeutic. When I say this out loud I think it sounds crazy. Should I stop?

-Ishia, 31, Omaha, Nebraska

Dear Fuck, Fight or Draw,

The first thing that comes to mind is, I hope you're not an ex-felon. There is a Federal Statute, which prescribes a 10-year maximum penalty for a previously convicted felon in possession of a firearm or ammunition. Thus, if you have a felony criminal record, STOP shooting right now and dispose of the weapon and ammunition forthwith. It's not worth it! (Remember **TI**). That being said, I will proceed with an answer to your question. Life can be extremely frustrating. Just about everyone finds or creates an outlet for their frustrations.

The average person finds relief from the day-to-day hardships of life and resulting stress by either fucking or fighting. I'm sure these most popular methods have some root in the fact that you can usually do either for free. However, you seem to have come upon a non-traditional means of release and satisfaction. So, in summary, as long as you're not an ex-felon and proper safety precautions are being followed, I think you are on to some good shit here. With your brand of pleasure one cannot get their head busted, STD'S, HIV/AIDS, unwanted pregnancies or end up in love with someone you can't stand. Sounds like a hell-of-a deal to me!

"Shoot first and ask questions later."   **--Folks**

Dear Player,

   I am an ex-addict and I'm wondering whether I should tell my doctor? At first, I didn't

think it was necessary. I underwent a minor procedure. They had a hard time medicating me. I still felt everything that they were doing to me, even after they gave me pain meds, and now I am re-thinking this whole thing. My main concern is that my doctor may treat me differently. Am I worried about the wrong thing?
-Valerie Davis, 44, Augusta, Ga

Dear Need a Doc without a Crock,

Like most things or events in life, the real is your best option. There are two persons to whom no one should ever lie or omit the truth from. Those persons are your doctor and your lawyer. Both of these people hold your life in their hands. Neither your doctor, nor your lawyer, can properly help you unless they have ALL of the information available. It's near impossible to fix anything or anyone if you don't know when, where or how it's broken.

However, believe it or not, lawyers and doctors are two of the most frequently lied to professionals in business. I don't get it. Your doctor will not know how to or what to treat you for, if he/she doesn't know everything about you, your medical history and behavior. The same applies to your attorney. A lawyer cannot properly represent you if he/she doesn't know exactly what's going on with you or why. Do you see what I'm saying?

Now, regarding the fact that your doctor may treat you differently if he or she is aware of your former status as a drug abuser; you are totally correct in your assessment that physicians become paranoid when treating former drug users/abusers. Thus, arises the need for even more realism on your part. You need to explain your entire medical history including the drug abuse. At the same time you need to explain that you are being totally honest, and in exchange you expect the same in return. Relay your desire for completely honest medical treatment. In the alternative, ask for the same treatment anyone else receives or the doctor's admission that he is unable to give such treatment based upon stereotyping.

This type of mutual honesty and realism will allow the doctor to either treat you fairly or allow you to find a physician that will. The bigger problem here is the manner in which doctors treat former drug addicted persons, which is a part of the reason that drug users or former drug users are not usually forth coming with drug-related information. The only way you can be assured of proper, unbiased medical treatment is through mutual honesty and respect between doctor and patient, as well as the patient's sincere desire to live well. A person's drug use/abuse, or lack thereof, should in no way impede or limit the quantity or quality of his/her medical treatment. Last, but certainly not least, the Hippocratic Oath does not provide a single exception to the duty of a doctor to human beings.

" Say no to drugs- not addicts."

--Folks

Dear Player,

I think my girl friend is crazy! We have filmed ourselves having sex. We have even filmed threesomes. Now my girl wants me to film her having sex with a German Shepherd! I don't know how to take this. What should I do?

-David Perkins, 29, Des Moines

Dear Your Girl Likes it "Doggie Style,"

I don't know what to tell you brother. This requires more game and understanding than I possess. Perhaps you should contact Michael Vick. I hear that he is an animal lover of sorts. One thing for sure, your girl has taken "Doggie Style" to the next level. Do not discount the fact that this kind of shit is worth a fortune on video…

"Dog Pound, or Pound the Dog? You call it. It's your girl." Best description of a "bitch" I've ever heard.

P.S. You may want to get tested for STDs, Maybe rabies? -- **Folks**

Dear Player,

I brought a used car from my neighbor and it completely broke down 3 weeks later. I want my brother to confront him, or should I?

-Mina Banes, 27, Chicago

Dear Bought a Lemon,

I feel your pain sister. I'm sure you would like to stick your shoe so far into your neighbor's ass that he would need to have it surgically removed. However, you will be hustling backwards on that one. Your neighbor will be able to have you arrested and incarcerated for assault. Incarceration will cost you even more money. You need to play past the sucker shit. You have already been played on. Don't play yourself. Sue your neighbor in small claims court under the Illinois Lemon Law. You will not need a lawyer in Small Claims Court. Your only cost will be a small filing fee. Of course, if you win your case your neighbor will not only have to pay you, he will have to pay the filing fee as well. You legally bought the car. Legally give it back. This is real game. Sue the bastard!

"Make that sucker pay."   **--Folks**

Dear Player,

My mom told me you could judge a person by their shoes. Is there any truth to that statement?

Dear Check Out Their Kicks & See How They Roll,

Absolutely! My grandfather imparted that same bit of knowledge to me as a teenager. My grandfather's version was expanded to include not only shoes but automobiles as well. Specifically, my grandfather said, "you can tell a lot about a man's character by the way he keeps his shoes and his car." This "advice" also included an explanation of the meaning of the statement. I was told "if a man did not shine his shoes or wash his car on a regular basis he was of low esteem or character." The logic was: that as important as your feet and shoes are to your ability to move about, if you buy cheap shoes or do not keep your shoes cleaned and shined you don't respect yourself. Of course, the same logic applies to one's vehicle as well. In turn, if one has such little respect for their own appearance or ability to move around, then that person is due no respect from others. If a person has no respect for themselves, what can you expect them to have for you?

"Keep your shoes and your car up to par." --**Folks**

Dear Player,

What is the definition of "player"? I've heard it refered to as people who have many that cater to them either with sex or other services. Then I read your column and got a different perspective, which I can't recall, but it didn't have anything to do with having a lot of sex. Can you help me out here?

-Traesha, 24, Henderson, NV

The Original White Folks

Dear Trae Who Wants to Know the Play,

You are right I did provide a definition for "player" some time ago. At the risk of being repetitious I will give you an expanded answer. First off, let me state that being a true player has nothing to do with having sex, how much you get or how many partners you have sex with. In fact, the least sexually motivated your thoughts are the better player you will become. Being a player requires the game and ability to rise above your circumstances by manipulating people, situations, circumstances and information to your advantage for financial gain. Such manipulation is done as a business or profession.

Players usually play organized game such as the con game, check writing, identity theft, pick pocketing, short changing, 3-card Monte, the greasy pea (shell game), slum jewelry, etc. These games are played according to a set of rules passed down from one generation of players to the next. The wannabe and uninformed brand of modern day player incorrectly believes that being a player has something to do with playing with their dicks. In truth, the more time and effort one puts into trying to get pussy, chasing his dick, the less time and effort he has left to perfect the skills necessary to obtain large sums of money in a short period of time. Chasing sexual favors is a sucker or trick activity. Calling one's self a player based upon his ability to have multiple sex partners is ludicrous. The proper name for such person is freak, not player. If you're fucking more than one girl and the girls don't know about each other, you are a cheater … not a player.

This is yet another new-age misuse of player's vocabulary. It's kind of like the rappers that call themselves pimps and players instead of rappers. Most rappers can't even play a musical instrument much less any real game. Most of them couldn't be a pimple on a pimp's ass. Most of these so-called Players are really "Payers". I trust that I have answered your question. I hope that I have also given the masses of young guys who call themselves or throw around the word player reason to rethink their position.

"Play game not pussy"   **--Folks**

Dear Player,

What's the deal with pimp cups? I've seen a lot of both famous pimps and rappers with them. I'm confused. I thought those cups were for pimps only.

-La Don Da P., 28, Compton, Ca

The Original White Folks

Dear What's Up With the Cup?

Honestly, I have to admit that I really don't know. There is a definite split among certain groups of pimps on the subject of whether to cup or not to cup. I will not attempt to speak for one side of the cup issue or the other. I can only give you my personal thoughts and observations on the subject. I don't know the philosophy or history behind the ownership of a pimp cup.

However, as you pointed out, a lot of rappers have these cups. In fact, some rappers have bejeweled gold and platinum "pimp cups." The first thing that comes to my mind is the question: What does a rapper (or any non Pimp) do with a "pimp cup?" Wouldn't that be kind of like me having a bra? I don't have anything to put in it.

The best I can do is to pass along some of the answers I have received to the pimp cup question. I have been told that it's a "fashion statement", a "pimp accessory", a means of being identified and a few other non-descript explanations.

There are a lot of unauthorized suckers, lames, clowns and buffoons carrying pimp cups around where ever they travel. These groups of people are attempting to make-up in flash what they lack in game. These guys also lack the common sense that the purchase of a pimp cup does not make you a pimp. I have been told that the cup is for pimps to put their drinks into. My response is that I can put my drink in a Styrofoam cup. If it's my cup, damn-it, it's a pimp cup! Additionally, if I am a pimp I don't need a cup, sign, banner or flag to be identified as a pimp. In over 40 years of having hos I have never once found a use for a cup in pimping! The butt naked truth is self-evident.

However, I don't subscribe to ownership of **a** pimp cup for a number of reasons. The above are but a few examples of why the line has been drawn in the sand between the cup holders and the non-cup holders. Obviously, I am not a cup holder. It doesn't work for me. There are those pimps whose ownership of a cup works for them, and for those brothers may the Pimp God bless them. However, pimp cups just don't work for me. All of the Pimps I know Pimp hos… not cups!

"I'm all for any game that works. I'm not hating on cups, but if *anyone* can have one, I don't want one."

NO CUPS, NO CANES, NO CAPES… JUST GAME!!

--Folks

Dear Player,

You have talked a ton of stuff about women and relationships. I just want to know, as a Player, what is the ideal woman for you?

-LaNissa, 27, Lee's Summit, MO

Dear Nissa,

Show me the right woman and I'll kissa. This question requires considerable thought as to which side of me you are asking it of. I'm currently retired from the game. However, as a lifetime player, I can only give you one answer... a player's answer.

We will begin with the ideal age. The age of the ideal woman ranges between 25 and 35 years old. I want her to be young enough to have the supple tight body of an athlete, yet old enough to have experienced some of real life's hard knocks. Someone who has bumped her head enough to realize that life is not all it should be or is supposed to be; but rather life **is** what it **is**.

I require an educated woman, not necessarily education of a formal nature. However, my woman needs to have, at a bare minimum, street survival skills that exceed the average. My logic here is if a woman reaches the age of 25 years or more and has not obtained either a formal education, vocational training or perfected some slick moves, she is not capable of understanding or learning the advanced game I will teach her. There has long been a misconception that women who get in the game are stupid. Contrary to popular lame belief, a woman has to be of above average intelligence to successfully participate in the game. Among other things game is the ability to skillfully manipulate people, situations and circumstances to one's financial advantage. So, you have to have skill, game and intelligence to do so.

My ideal woman needs a realistic outlook on life, love and sexuality, with the emphasis on the sexuality. My woman would need to be sexually liberated in order to do all that may be required to succeed in life. It may become necessary to sell pussy, strip or work an escort service. Notwithstanding the enormous appetite I have for 3-somes and beyond.

A woman with the right understanding of game can get the average man to do astronomical "favors" for them. A woman with proper instruction and polished game can accomplish these types of feats based upon a man's idea that he "may" get laid or a promise at best. Of course, sometimes the mere promise simply will not turn the trick, (Pun intended).

Now, we come to physical appearance and attributes. I prefer intelligence and game over booty, boobs and blowjobs. An ass resembling two basketballs, a double D cup bra, a small waist and a pretty face all make doing business a pleasure. However, given a choice, I would take an ugly woman with intelligence over a pretty woman with booty, boobs and no brains every time.

Class and style again, are attributes much more desirable than boobs and booty. A woman that can speak, dress and conduct herself with a sense of decorum has value far greater than a half dozen hood stars with famous butts, boobs and Gucci bags.

In summary, I need a woman that has the game, heart and intelligence to understand and play sophisticated game; with the class and style to pull it off without question. The sexual appeal to make a sucker's dick hard as Chinese arithmetic from across the street; The game to sell a snowball to an Eskimo and the charm to talk a nun into a 3-some; A realistic understanding of men and the power of pussy over them. The ability to listen and follow the voice of experience and wisdom verses operating on guesswork, common misconceptions and misunderstanding of what's real. I need a woman who is capable of becoming all of the following:

Ask a player

CEO of a corporation
Check writer
Corporate executive
Con game player
Credit card scam artist
Expert marksman
Identity thief
Pick- pocket
Prostitute
Professional escort
Stripper
Short change artist
Butcher
Baker and a
Candle -stick maker

These are but a few of the important traits I would look for in a woman. The ideal woman for me, as a player only has to be slick enough and committed enough to be capable to learn all of the above and the finesse to pull it all off. It takes a rare, special breed of woman to fit into this category. At the risk of being repetitious I want to reiterate that I have retired from the game; but my appetite for excellence in women has not.

"The desire to do it is not enough. This is not Nike, you can't "just do it", you have to be good at it or get instruction from someone that is.   **--Folks**

Dear Player,

I am allergic to latex, having sex with a man wearing a latex condom causes severe burning, itching and swelling in my vaginal area. The thought of unprotected sex scares me. What do I do?

-Jennifer Norris, Lansing, IL

Dear Damned If You Do or Dead If You Don't,

Whatever you do, don't have unprotected sex! Some 6 million men and women in this country alone share your allergy to latex. I'm going to provide some interesting information for you: Latex condoms are said to contain contaminants, which are linked to cancer, sterility and tumors in fallopian tubes. The spermicides used on many latex condoms are believed to undermine the hormonal system in both men and women and are linked to both breast and prostate cancers. These spermicides are also associated with low sperm count in men.

In direct answer to your question, you have two options to get your groove back:

1. your partner can strap on a latex condom and cover it with a lambskin condom. This move protects you from latex as well as provides you both with STD, HIV, AIDS, HPV and pregnancy

protection. Lambskin condoms have tiny holes in them because they are made from living tissue. Therefore, lambskin condoms alone provide little protection. Your partner may find this double condom move less than ideal for his pleasure.

2. The good news is that there is another alternative, which does not require your partner to get "all dressed up." The word is polyurethane. Polyurethane/plastic condoms are available through the Avanti and Trojan manufacturing companies at a cost of about $11.99 - $14.99 per dozen. You can purchase or at least order these alternative condoms from most major drug stores. Polyurethane does not affect persons that are allergic to latex, while providing as much protection without the contaminants. You can scratch your itch without having an additional itch to scratch.

Keep in mind that studies have shown that the use of condoms is only 85% to 90% effective as a preventative measure against STD'S, HIV/AIDS, HPV or pregnancy. Personally, I wouldn't fuck the Virgin Mary without a condom. No disrespect to God.

"Get it in where you can fit it in"   **--Folks**

Dear Readers,

In an attempt to provide an adequate answer to a previous question, I wish to expand my answer to lasts weeks question regarding the ideal woman for me as a player. Last weeks answer listed the basic skills, capabilities and qualifications for a true player's ideal woman. This week I will conclude my list of requirements:

You see, a real polished player will not only have occasion to be down and dirty in the streets but players also conduct business in 5 star hotels, restaurants and boardrooms. Therefore, both a player and his woman are required to be able to dress and have proper etiquette/decorum for such occasions. The ability to wear an evening gown, properly accessorize and know the difference between a dinner fork, a salad fork, and a dessert fork are imperative. In conjunction with these skills comes the additional ability to carry on intelligent, articulate current affairs conservations. In other words, a player's woman has to be able to wear the totally real hat of a player as well as the plastic contrived hat of "high society". Pip pip and all that rot ole girl.

This may sound like a near impossible laundry list of qualifications. However, any true polished player will eventually take his game from the bedrooms to the boardrooms. When this transformation occurs a player's woman has to be a reflection of him, all he stands for and represents at all times. This is the computer age. Street game and street players are fast becoming extinct, out dated and out of style. More and more there are either over-dressed or under dressed, inarticulate lames, suckers, clowns and buffoons claiming to be pimps, players and ambassadors of game. Meanwhile, real players are taking their game to the next level, going to places no players have gone before. You see, real players have the game to envision the future and see the handwriting on the wall. "Heap see, but few know."

What pimps and players did 20 or 30 years ago are not necessarily slick moves in this day and age. Hey, this is not 20 or 30 years ago, this is the computer age, see what I'm saying? I trust that I have provided the finishing touches on the description of an ideal woman for me as a player. I've used this quote before but it seems appropriate here.

"You cannot soar like an eagle when you are surrounded by turkeys"   --Folks

Dear Player,

My little sister and a couple of her friends all say they would like to "do" a pimp. What's up with these young girls' (17-19) fascination with pimps?

-Zacory Pell, 25, Tulsa, OK

Dear Your Sister is Hot for Game,

Your sister and her friend's fascination for pimps is born out of at least one of several common psychological syndromes. Number one on the list is the star-like lifestyle pimps lead. These girls have the star attraction syndrome. Then we come to the forbidden fruit syndrome. Pimps are known to have an entourage of pretty sexy women. Therefore, if a woman or girl is able to attract the sexual attention of a pimp her ego, self-confidence, and self-esteem will receive a major boost. Certainly not the least of considerations here is that if pimps can sexually satisfy women who have sex with men as a profession they must have phenomenal sex appeal and sexual moves. Women usually feel that they simply must "get themselves some of that." I think this behavior can be likened to a moth drawn to a flame or maybe even the way some people are drawn to drugs and alcohol. Groupies, Star fuckers?

"Maybe there is some truth to the long standing myth that pimps have magical powers and mystical sex appeal"

--Folks

Dear Player,

I agreed to a three-some between myself, my man and another woman. I even recruited the other woman. Afterwards, I expressed my desire to have another three-some but this time I wanted a man as the third person. My man looked at me like he wanted to slap me silly. Why was it OK to fulfill his fantasy but not mine?
-Anajaha, 28, Fargo, ND

Dear Unfilled Fantasy,

As a woman you should be aware of one of the most fragile things in the universe... the male ego. You obviously fall short of this knowledge. Men have perfect understanding when it comes to their desire for 3-somes and strange or different partners for sex. However, when it comes to a man's understanding of his woman's desire to have a 3-

some involving two men his understanding ratio is zero. This is one of those situations where the double standard does not work in women's favor.
I had a question a few months back similar to yours. I will give you a similar answer as well. If you have a serious itch regarding your desire for a 3-some with yourself and two men; do not have your man as one of the men to scratch it. Between men's egos, macho issues and the sense of possession of women, you don't stand a chance in hell wearing gasoline drawers of getting your man on board. My suggestion to you is to find yourself a couple of guys who do not know you or your man. You can scratch your itch, call it a good day at the office and avoid a mountain of bullshit that will be heaped upon you. Always use condoms; they are better than American Express, never leave home without em!

Keep in mind that finding two men that will be comfortable naked in bed together may not be as simple as it sounds. Exercise caution, being a freak in this day and age can be dangerous unless you are a trained professional.

"If one is good, two has got to be better. But sometimes three can be a crowd"   **--Folks**

Dear Player,

    I am confused. A lot of white people claim not to care for the black or other non-white races of people. I have noticed that every time the sun comes out white people are out in droves trying to get a tan. Is dark skin only beautiful if one of them is wearing it?

-Abdul Nasir Rahim, 31, Chicago

Dear Confused Brother,

    Actually, you have answered your own question. A number of white people like the color... on them. Many have a kind of love/hate relationship with dark skin. They love the color but tend to think very little of people that wear it naturally. I'm sure they are not happy with the fact that they have to risk skin cancer and a host of other related problems to achieve brown skin. Think about it... Cosmetic companies sell millions if not billions of dollars worth of bronzing gels, suntan lotions, sunscreen and other related products to white people every summer. There are multi-millions of dollars spent in tanning salons year- round. The darker skin look has become so appealing to white people that an entire industry was created just to maintain the tanned look for this group of people all year. (Tanning

salons) They acknowledge the fact that their skin looks healthy, sexy and desirable with color.
"As soul brother #1, James Brown said: "Say it loud, I'm black and I'm proud!"   **--Folks**

Dear Player,

I have heard my uncle talk about someone being a "professional friend". Exactly what does that mean?

-Pamela Massey, 25, Pittsburgh

Dear Wanna Know about the Buddy Plan,

A professional friend is someone who devotes all of their time sucking up to someone with money and/or fame in the name of friendship. These persons are labeled professionals because:

1. It's all they do for a living
2. They are good at it
3. They like what they do

These people live vicariously through someone else's fame and fortune. In other words, a professional friend can claim fame without putting in the **work. See what I'm saying? Kind of like a sidekick** or a vice president, he's just there to co-sign whatever the president says. Can you spell professional ass-kisser? Yeah, that.

"A Professional friend... he's your friend whether you need one or not."

--Folks

Dear Player,

I am a single mother of a boy. I keep hearing that a woman cannot teach a boy how to be a man. Is that true?

-Avis Robinson, 26, Lima, OH

Dear Mom,

Thank you, on behalf of your son, for having the wherewithal to seek the truth on this subject. This is a rare move indeed. To answer your question, it's true. A woman **cannot** teach a boy to be a man. There are so many complicated steps necessary to make that transition I can't begin to list them. Suffice to say a boy learns true manhood from men. A woman can only teach a boy to be what a woman thinks a man should be. Kind of like a fish teaching a baby bird to fly. He can't, because a fish has never flown. Can an electrician teach someone to be a plumber? Yeah... like that. A boy needs to drive a nail, turn a screw, lay a brick, cut down a tree, fix a car, change a tire and the list goes on to infinity and beyond. Then there are those all-important sex talks. He needs to be taught respect for women as well as the games woman play. You cannot duplicate or substitute the wisdom that comes from living life as a man. Therefore, you are incapable of passing on this all important knowledge to your man-child because you do not possess it. It takes a whole village to raise a child.

"If you don't get yourself a man, get one for your son's sake"

--Folks

Dear Readers,

I want to begin by expanding my answer to last week's question from the single mother. This single parent expressed concern regarding a women's ability to teach a boy to be a man. After giving that question additional thought, I decided

to provide more insight. I merely scratched the surface last week.

Boys learn to be men by example and association with men. Of course, a boy's father is the man he sees, or at least is supposed to see the most frequently. Therefore, the boys with fathers in their lives often imitate them. The father is the male child's role model. When the father is not present in a boy's life the slack can be taken up by brothers or uncles, maybe even cousins. However, when there are no other close male relatives, mothers can potentially ruin boy's lives.

Women have a tendency to attempt to teach their male children to be what they think the ideal man should be. The incredible error in that train of thought is that it's all done from a female perspective. You see, if a man does everything exactly like a woman wants it done he's not really a man; he will be more like a "bitch ass man".

This may sound a little harsh but it's the butt naked truth. Some women with no man in their lives also have a tendency to bash men. Therefore, boys grow up hearing a lot of adverse comments about men. A number of these boys begin to view men as a source of pain for their mothers. No child wants to see a parent in pain. Thus, some boys may seriously question whether or not they want to join the ranks of the givers of pain. (Man). You see where this can go?

Boys learn to be men in the same way any other person learns to do anything of importance. You learn to be an electrician from electricians. You learn plumbing from plumbers. You learn to be a politician from politicians and you know how the rest of it goes... The bottom line here is that boys learn to be men from men. However, in view of the alarming number of absentee fathers, a number of our young men are being raised by women and other children. These factors contribute greatly to the reason for large numbers of "down low" brothers; The lack of respect for manhood or much of anything else, rude, obnoxious behavior; high school dropouts; criminal activity; drug and alcohol abuse; domestic violence and the list goes on. My point being that if a male does not learn how to be a man from a man with realistic life experiences he will likely become something less than man.

You men that are fathers... act like it! Spend some time (and money) with your children. We need to raise more real men. Hopefully, you women do not take offense to what I am saying here. I am in no way trying to bash the single mothers. Believe me, I know you are doing the absolute best you can with what you have to work with. It is my purpose and intent to provide you sisters with an honest, well thought out male perspective on this issue. I hope that being armed with this information you will have cause, and a sense of purpose to build-in additional considerations when shopping for a man. What I'm saying is that you can't give these boys all they need because you simply do not possess it. It's not on you at this point... It's on the "baby daddies", boy-friends and relatives.

-"I really want to see our young people make it."

--Folks

Dear Player,

The government is trying to pass a law that would make it illegal to wear your pants below your waist. I think this is a set up to arrest & convict more of our young black men! What do you think? The criminal justice system is definitely not designed to be in our favor. These young men don't realize that showing your underwear is indecent. My son is 14 and wears his pants so low I can see his butt crack. I don't think he realizes how serious this is? What can I tell him to make him see it my way?

-Shanavia Smith, Baltimore, Md.

The Original White Folks

Dear Trying to Get the Slack Over junior's Crack,

First of all, the wearing of one's pants on one's waist is not "your way." It's the proper way. That being said you are 14 years late for teaching your son proper or socially acceptable behavior. I am willing to bet that your male child's father is not in his life or yours. I don't know what you've been doing the last 14 years but you need to step your mommy game up. I agree that the system is geared towards incarcerating as many young black men as possible. However unfair and unjust the system may be, there are some things that cannot be blamed on "the man" or "the system". Some of our problems arise from the lack of plain ole "home training" (manners; social graces). We need to stop giving our children to the system! Let them work to try and get them. Children are like banks... The more you put in, the more you can get out with interest. If you don't put anything in you cannot get anything out. Please take every spare moment you have to teach your child what's real and what is important in order to live a safe and productive life.

The lack of "home training" is a big part of the reason that nearly 2 million people are in jails and prisons. A lot of our youth are raising themselves for the most part. If you are having trouble raising your children ask for help. Get a man who cares, ask older people. Older people have a lifetime of knowledge and experience and most are more than willing to share it if requested to do so. Think of the impact that untrained uneducated children have on the future of our people and society in general. What will these teen children teach their children eight or ten years from now? Hopefully you are getting a look at the big picture here. Stop whatever it is you've been doing with your time and shape the life and life-style of your child before it's too late.

"A child is a terrible thing to waste"   --**Folks**

Dear Player,

I just found out that my husband of 15 years possibly has a 17 years old daughter he never knew about. He ended up discovering this days before a big family reunion. I was present at the reunion and was the last to know. At the reunion this "mystery woman" showed up and I was the only person that didn't know who she was. Finally my curiosity got the best of me and I asked my husband who she was. He said it was his high school girlfriend's daughter. I joked that she looked a lot like him and could be his. He replied that according to his mother she just might be, and that's basically how I was told about her. I feel really betrayed and hurt he didn't tell me as soon as it was brought to his attention. He told me he didn't want to tell me before the event because he didn't want the "drama", especially since he hadn't had a DNA test to confirm paternity.

I don't like the idea of this woman, (girl) intruding in our affairs. She is almost eighteen, so he won't be financially responsible for her in just a few months anyway. I don't want to be selfish but I am really disgusted with the whole thing. Why didn't he tell me when he first found out? Should I leave him over this? I don't want to but what do I tell OUR kids? How can I accept this love child without feeling resentment?

Eddie Mae Matthews 48, Flint, MI

Dear Can't Handle The Truth,

It is apparent to me right off the rip why he didn't tell you. The first two things that came to your mind were 1. Financial responsibility 2. "Should I leave him?" Damn-it woman, we are talking about a child in need of guidance, direction, understanding and most of all a father. This child is a part of your husband and is your children's sister like it or not. What did she do to you?

Last, but certainly not least, this young lady was conceived more than two years before you and your hubby were married. How uncaring, unfeeling and cold hearted can you be? Are you still wondering why he never told you about his daughter? Did it occur to you that you are intruding on her life and preventing a healthy father/daughter relationship? Your husband is connected to his daughter by blood. He is connected to you by a piece of paper. Maybe you should re-think your position here. After all, he had this child before you were a part of his life. Which one of you supplies a pain in your husband's ass? So, which one of you would be the one to go if given a choice? Now, do you really want the child out of your life?

"Be careful what you wish for"   --**Folks**

Dear Player,

My future mother in law put a relaxer in my 3 year old daughter's hair, took her to get her ears pierced, and dresses her in grown up looking clothes. I am furious, she is using my daughter as a dress up doll. Every time she takes my daughter out she comes back with something new. She never consults me before she does this. They went to a spa last week! I'd like to experience some firsts with my own child. My

fiancé says that I should stop over-reacting and that his mother is only trying to help. What's your take on this?

Evelyn Montgomery, 26, San Bernadino, Ca

Dear Got an Out-law for an In-law,

Sounds like your "baby daddy momma" has very little regard for your wishes. It also appears that your daughter has a ghetto granny who suffers from acute hoochie syndrome. I have a question for you. Have you expressed your dissatisfaction regarding these "hood-life" expeditions directly with granny? Nowhere in your writing do you make reference to a direct conversation with grandma ghetto. I don't know what you've done or not done to create such a lack of respect for you by this woman. Maybe it's simply a lack of decorum or common sense on her part.

Whatever the case, you need to stand up and be counted on this issue. Express your feelings and desire to be consulted. Make it known that if your wishes are not respected there will be no visits period! If you suspend visiting privileges you will have no hoochie headaches. So, simply tell your soon to be in-law/out-law that you don't like the way she does business and either the violations or the visits will stop...point blank! Visitation is a privilege that has to be earned.

"You have to stand for something or fall for anything"

--Folks

Dear Player,

My brother works for me in my private trucking business. He is always late with shipments and is constantly picking up "lot lizards". I told him he's playing with fire and it's starting to make my company look bad. I can work with him being late but I can't deal with the hoes. I am about to give him a pink slip. He says I'm hating. Am I?

Alfred Armstead, St. Paul, MN

Dear Bashing Your Brother,

You are worried about the wrong thing here. Although your brother's behavior with "lot lizards" (hoes) may be disgusting or even hazardous to his health... that's his dick and if he wants to shovel coal with it what the hell do you care? You should be concerned about your brother's tardiness in regard to picking up or delivering shipments. Now, that's something that affects both you and your business.

Therefore, if I were you, I would concentrate my efforts on getting brother man to tighten up his time schedule. I cannot for the life of me see how your brother playing Dick Dastardly and having a stink fest for his "Johnson" has a single thing to do with you or your business. I don't believe your customers know or care what your brother does with his dick. They want prompt pick-up and delivery. Keep on truckin!

"Mind your truckin... Not his fuckin!"

--Folks

Send video or written questions to: Askaplayer@gmail.com. Your question may be featured on youtube or in one of our books. Note: Due to the number of questions we receive, we cannot guarantee a response to all of your questions. We try.

See also: www.youtube.com/
Originalwhitefolks
Filmed at GFE studios, Atlanta, Ga.

COMING SOON!

ASK A PLAYER

VOLUME II

Other books by this author:

**ORIGINAL GAME, Interview with
an old school player.**

**This book has everything you ever wanted
to know about Game, but was afraid to
ask, or didn't know who to ask. Real Game
from a genuine Player.**

**Available on: www.Barnes&Noble.com
www.Amazon.com**